A Special Issue of the
European Journal of Developmental Psychology

Social cognition during infancy

Guest Editors

Vincent M. Reid
Durham University, UK

Tricia Striano
University of Leipzig, Germany

Willem Koops
Utrecht University, The Netherlands

Routledge
Taylor & Francis Group
LONDON AND NEW YORK

First published 2007 by Psychology Press

Published 2018 by Routledge
2 Park Square, Milton Park, Abingdon, Oxon OX14 4RN
52 Vanderbilt Avenue, New York, NY 10017

First issued in paperback 2018

Routledge is an imprint of the Taylor & Francis Group, an informa business

British Library Cataloguing in Publication Data
A catalogue record for this book is available from the British Library

Cover design by Jim Wilkie
Typeset in the UK by KnowledgeWorks Global Limited, Southampton

ISSN 1740-5629
ISBN 13: 978-1-138-87773-3 (pbk)
ISBN 13: 978-1-84169-832-8 (hbk)

Contents

EUROPEAN JOURNAL OF DEVELOPMENTAL PSYCHOLOGY
2007, 4 (1), 1

Social cognition during infancy: Introduction

Our knowledge of infant social cognition has advanced rapidly over the past few years. It is now known that infants systematically engage in joint attention activities, detect intentional structure within action, and use others' emotions and eye gaze to guide their own actions and evaluation of the environment. Infants even take a rational stance toward observed actions. These various skills point to an early capacity to predict other's goals and future mental states.

What is not currently well known is the early developmental trajectory of these skills; how they relate to each other and what aspects of person perception are foundational for other aspects of cognition, such as the relationship between action perception and action production. This special issue is primarily based on work presented at the dual symposia on early social cognition at the XXII European Conference on Developmental Psychology in Tenerife in August 2005.

From fundamental structural processing of human movement, through to the ability to segment action sequences, infancy research is only now addressing the issue of social cognition on a variety of cognitive fronts. This special issue has been designed to cover broad areas of social-cognitive development in order that we can build a more cohesive picture of the diversity within this area of developmental psychology. This issue seeks to outline and discuss changes in early development in terms of infant behavior that may suggest how an infant with limited experience may nonetheless identify and attribute to other humans a privileged social-cognitive status. This special issue has been a success on this front and also in its timeliness.

Vincent Reid, Tricia Striano and Willem Koops

DOI: 10.1080/17405620601005606

EUROPEAN JOURNAL OF DEVELOPMENTAL PSYCHOLOGY
2007, 4 (1), 2–13

The perception of facial expressions in newborns

Teresa Farroni
University of Padua, Italy, and Birkbeck College, University of London, UK

Enrica Menon and Silvia Rigato
University of Padua, Italy

Mark H. Johnson
Birkbeck College, University of London, UK

The ability of newborns to discriminate and respond to different emotional facial expressions remains controversial. We conducted three experiments in which we tested newborns' preferences, and their ability to discriminate between neutral, fearful, and happy facial expressions, using visual preference and habituation procedures. In the first two experiments, no evidence was found that newborns discriminate, or show a preference between, a fearful and a neutral face. In the third experiment, newborns looked significantly longer at a happy facial expression than a fearful one. We raise the possibility that this preference reflects experience acquired over the first few days of life. These results show that at least some expressions are discriminated and preferred in newborns only a few days old.

INTRODUCTION

The ability of infants to detect, discriminate, and process facial expressions has been debated for some time (Darwin, 1872; Ekman, Friesen, & Ellworth,

---

Correspondence should be addressed to Teresa Farroni, Centre for Brain and Cognitive Development, School of Psychology, Birkbeck College, University of London, Malet Street, London WC1E 7HX, UK. E-mail: t.farroni@bbk.ac.uk

This work was supported by the MRC (Programme Grant G97 15587) to MJ and by Welcome Trust (073985/Z/03/Z) to TF.

The authors thank the parents and infants who participated in the study, Stefano Massaccesi for the help with the software, Tobias Grossman for discussion, and Katiuschia Pastrello for help in testing the infants. The authors are deeply indebted to the nursing staff at the Pediatric Unit of the Hospital of Monfalcone for their collaboration.

DOI: 10.1080/17405620601046832

1972). In recent years this debate has been enhanced by evidence from adult cognitive neuroscience studies supporting the idea of a "quick and dirty" brain route for detecting some facial expressions that modulates the slower and more detailed cortical analysis of facial information (Adolphs & Tranel, 2003; Adolphs et al., 2005; de Gelder, 2006; Johnson, 2005). Specifically, this rapid route may depend on low spatial frequency information and be mediated by subcortical structures such as the superior colliculus, pulvinar, and amygdala (see Johnson, 2005). Given the lack of maturity in the cerebral cortex of the newborn human infant, one possibility is that this putative "quick and dirty" route guides the responses of newborns to some facial expressions, as well as orienting them to neutral faces in their visual environment (Johnson, 2005).

Many studies have been conducted on the development of the recognition of facial expressions during infancy (see De Haan & Nelson, 1998, for a review). Nevertheless, no clear conclusions can be drawn, and many questions remain. The first question concerns which expressions can be discriminated in the first few days after birth, and whether there is a particular expression that is preferred over others. A second question concerns what information is used by the infants to guide their preference. A third question that remains is at which age infants start to discriminate between different facial expressions.

While studies have mapped the development of the recognition of facial expressions during infancy and childhood (e.g., Kotsoni, De Haan, & Johnson, 2001), the issue of whether newborns can detect facial expressions has remained controversial. For example, Field, Woodson, Greenberg, and Cohen (1982, 1983) presented evidence that newborns can match their own facial expressions to a model face showing happiness, surprise, or sadness. However, an attempt to replicate these results with an improved procedure designed to eliminate experimenter error or unintentional bias failed to confirm the earlier report (Kaitz, Meschulach-Sarfaty, Auerbach, & Eidelman, 1988). Kaitz and colleagues showed newborns live faces that displayed different facial expressions or tongue protrusion. Two coders, blind as to the facial gesture being displayed, observed the newborn and coded their mouth and eye movements. These authors did not find evidence for selective imitation of emotional facial expressions since the newborns' facial movements did not vary with the different modelled expressions, and the observers were unable to guess the modelled expression by viewing the infants' faces. Importantly, this was not due to the sensitivity of the technique since significant evidence of matching to modelled tongue protrusion was found.

Given that newborns' ability to discriminate facial expressions remains controversial, we conducted three experiments in which we ascertained newborns' preferences, and ability to discriminate between, neutral, fearful, and happy facial expressions.

EXPERIMENT 1

Evidence from adult cognitive neuroscience indicates that fearful faces may maximally engage rapid and subcortical processing (Adolphs & Tranel, 2003; Adolphs et al., 2005). Given the possibility of unique processing of this facial expression, it is possible that newborns would be maximally sensitive to faces that display fear. In addition, the fearful expression contains wide eyes and an open mouth, and may therefore represent an enhancement of the features that orient newborns toward faces in general (Johnson, 2005). Thus, it is possible that the mechanisms that ensure that newborns orient toward faces (Johnson, Dziurawiec, Ellis, & Morton, 1991) and faces with direct gaze (Farroni, Csibra, Simion, & Johnson, 2002), may also cause them to preferentially orient to faces displaying fear. Such a preference has previously been observed in older infants (Nelson & Dolgin, 1985). An alternative possibility is that newborns, like older infants, find fearful faces aversive, and will thus display a preference for a neutral expression. Thus, in Experiment 1, we tested newborn infants to establish if they have a spontaneous preference for fearful versus neutral facial expressions.

Participants

Twenty-five normal, healthy, full-term newborns were selected from the maternity ward of the Pediatric Unit of the Hospital of Monfalcone. Eight babies were excluded from the final sample for various reasons. Four changed state during the experiment, one baby showed a strong side bias (they turned more than 85% of the time in one direction), and three others were excluded due to technical errors.

The 17 babies that completed the study met the screening criteria of normal delivery, a birth-weight between 2700 and 4270 g, and an Apgar score of at least 8 at 5 minutes. All were healthy and free of any known neurological or ocular abnormality. They were tested after the first 24 hours of life, the range of ages at time of test being from 24–96 hours postnatal (mean age of 46 hours). The testing took place during the hour proceeding the scheduled feeding time, if the baby was awake and in an alert state. Informed consent was obtained from the parents.

Apparatus and stimuli

The infants sat on the adult's lap 35 cm distant from a translucent screen. The baby holder was not actively involved in the experiment, was unaware of the hypothesis being tested in the experiment, and was not one of the authors. The newborn's eye level was aligned to the centre of the screen at the same level as the eyes of the faces. A video camera focused on the infant's face allowing the experimenter to monitor their eye movements. Infants were shown two pictures of the same person's face, one on the right and one on the left of the centre of the screen. One of the faces had a neutral face (no emotion) and the other had a fearful expression; both faces had a straight head and direct gaze (see Figure 1). Two different identity faces were used, but each newborn saw only one of them (randomly assigned, face (a) or face (b)). The faces were of different ethnic origin in order to allow us to generalize the results obtained. Face (a) subtended a visual angle of 20.2×31.1 degrees, and the external contour of the eyes 4.1×1.6 degrees in the case of neutral face and 4.1×2.8 degrees in the case of the fearful face (e.g., life-size as viewed from 35 cm distance). Face (b) subtended a visual angle of 19.5×32.7 degrees, and the external contour of the eyes 4.9×1.6 degrees in the case of neutral face and 4.5×2.6 degrees in the case of the

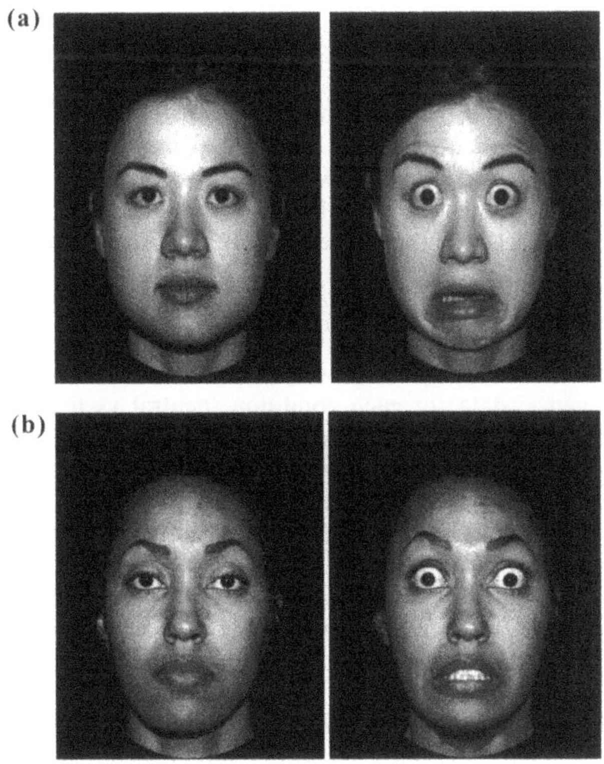

Figure 1. Stimuli used in Experiment 1. Half of the newborns saw photographic images of one face identity (a) and the other half saw the other face (b).

fearful face. In both stimuli the pupil was 1 cm in diameter. The two faces were 15.5 cm apart.

Procedure

Once the newborn was seated in front of the screen, as soon as she/he fixated the centre of the screen, the experimenter (who watched the newborn's eyes via a video monitor system) initiated a trial and presented the faces on the screen. The faces remained on for as long as the infant fixated on one of them (infant-control procedure). When the infants shifted their gaze away from the display for more than 10 s, the experimenter removed the faces and presented the next trial. In the second trial the location of the neutral and fear faces was reversed. Two trials were presented to the newborn with one left-to-right-reversal. This procedure has previously been used with newborns (e.g., Valenza, Simion, Macchi Cassia, & Umiltà, 1996). Two pseudo-random presentation sequences were used in which half of the infants saw a neutral face to the right and half to the left. Videotapes of the baby's eye movements throughout the trial were subsequently analysed by two coders blind as to the location of direct and averted gaze faces. The coders recorded, separately for each stimulus and each trial, the number of orienting responses and the total fixation time (interrater reliability for 10% of the total participants, Cohen's kappa = .88 for the duration of fixation and .90 for the number of orientations). While the coders could see the corneal reflection of the stimulus face (to help establish fixation), they could not see the details of the face, and they were blind as to expression being displayed.

Results and discussion

Preliminary statistical analyses showed no effects of order of presentation. As a consequence, data for each condition (neutral vs fearful face) were collapsed across this factor.

Two separate parametric tests were performed to compare the average total fixation time for each stimulus (neutral face vs fearful face) and the number of orientations in direction of each stimulus. Newborns did not show a significant difference in the total looking time at the neutral face ($M = 51.7$ s, $SD = 27.9$) or at the fearful face ($M = 43.4$ s, $SD = 16.9$), and they did not orient more frequently to either of the two facial expressions ($M = 20.35$, $SD = 7.2$ for the neutral face, and $M = 17.41$, $SD = 7.5$ for the fearful face).

Thus, in Experiment 1, newborns did not show any preference for one facial expression over the other. The next question that we investigated is whether newborns are able to discriminate between a face with a fearful expression and a neutral face.

EXPERIMENT 2

One obvious reason why newborns show no preference between fearful and neutral facial expressions is that they may not be able to discriminate between these stimuli. Alternatively, they may be able to discriminate between them, but they categorize and process them in the same way. Further, visual habituation may sometimes be a more sensitive technique for revealing newborn perceptual processing than preference measures. Therefore, in Experiment 2, we sought to determine whether newborns could discriminate between the two stimuli presented in Experiment 1 using a visual habituation and discrimination method.

Participants

Seventeen normal, healthy, full-term newborns were selected from the maternity ward of the Pediatric Unit of the Hospital of Monfalcone. Three babies were excluded from the final sample for various reasons. Two changed state during the experiment, one baby showed a strong side bias (they turned more than 85% of the time in one direction). The final sample consisted of 14 newborns. All of them met the screening criteria of normal delivery, a birth weight between 2610 and 3920 g, and a 5 minute Apgar score above 8. Infants were tested after the first 24 hours of life. Their ages at the time of testing ranged from approximately 24 to 120 hours ($M = 56$ h). Informed consent was obtained from the parents.

Apparatus and stimuli

The apparatus and the stimuli were the same as these used in Experiment 1. During the habituation phase the newborns viewed pairs of identical face stimuli (same identity, same expression, one on the right and one on the left of the screen) with either a neutral expression or a fearful expression. During the test phase the two different expressions of the same identity face were presented bilaterally.

Procedure

The experiment was carried out using a visual habituation technique with the infant-control procedure (Slater, Morison, Town, & Rose, 1985). The newborn was judged to have habituated when, from the fourth fixation on, the sum of any three consecutive fixations was 50% or less than the total of the first three fixations. When the habituation criterion was reached, the stimulus was automatically turned off and a preference test phase started.

The habituation with one of the two expressions was followed by a preference test in which a preference could be expressed between the familiar face expression (either neutral or fearful face) and the novel one. The two test stimuli were shown in both left and right positions, the positions being reversed from the first to the second presentation.

Results and discussion

During the habituation phase, the average total fixation time was 70.2 s ($SD = 21.6$) for the neutral expression and 72.0 s ($SD = 27.4$) for the fearful expression.

During the test phase, to test whether the infants were able to recognize the face seen previously, a 2×2 ANOVA was performed with the Stimulus Condition (familiar vs novel) and the Order Presentation (first vs second presentation) as within-subject factors. Only the order of presentation was significant, showing that the newborns looked more during the first presentation than the second one, independently of the stimulus condition, $F(1, 13) = 9.413$, $p = .009$. Most importantly, no significant effect of stimulus condition or interaction was found, showing that the newborns were unable to discriminate between the neutral and fearful faces.

Experiments 1 and 2 revealed no evidence that newborns prefer or discriminate fearful from neutral facial expressions. One possibility is that these stimuli are simply not discriminable to newborns. However, given their sensitivity to direction of eye gaze (Farroni et al., 2002) and individual identity (Pascalis & de Schonen, 1994; Pascalis, de Schonen, Morton, Deruelle, & Fabre-Grenet, 1995), this seems unlikely. A more intriguing possibility is that fearful and neutral expressions are discriminable, but are processed or categorized in the same way by newborns. This could be consistent with a perceptual learning view pointing to their lack of experience with fearful expressions, or with the view that fearful and neutral expressions both equally engage the primitive face detection mechanisms underlying their behaviour (Johnson, 2005).

EXPERIMENT 3

Since the first experiments failed to provide evidence for discrimination or preference between different facial expressions in newborns, in the next experiment we decided to compare the fearful expression to a happy facial expression. This comparison was selected for two reasons. First, contrasting fearful with happy may increase the perceptual distance between the stimuli as compared to the earlier pair. Second, although our healthy newborns had very limited experience of faces, this experience was likely to include happy and smiling faces.

Participants

Twenty-one normal, healthy, full-term newborns were selected from the maternity ward of the Pediatric Unit of the Hospital of Monfalcone. Nine babies were excluded from the final sample for various reasons. Five changed state during the experiment, three were excluded due to technical errors, and one for being more than two standard deviations beyond the mean average fixation time. The final sample consisted of 12 newborns. All of them met the screening criteria of normal delivery, a birth weight between 2300 and 4480 g, and a 5 minute Apgar score above 8. Infants were tested after the first 24 hours of life. Their ages at the time of testing ranged from approximately 31 to 87 hours ($M = 54$ h). Informed consent was obtained from the parents.

Apparatus and stimuli

The apparatus was the same as that used in Experiment 1. Infants were shown two pictures of the same person's face, one on the right and one on the left of the centre of the screen. One of the faces had a happy expression and the other had a fearful expression, both with a straight head and direct gaze (see Figure 2). The face subtended a visual angle of 19.5×32.7 degrees, and the external contour of the eyes 4.5×2.3 degrees in the case of the happy face and 4.5×2.6 degrees in the case of the fearful face (e.g., life-size as viewed from 30–35 cm distance). In both stimuli the pupil was 0.7 cm in diameter. The two stimuli were 15.5 cm apart.

Procedure

The procedure was the same as that used in Experiment 1. The coders recorded, separately for each stimulus and each trial, the number of

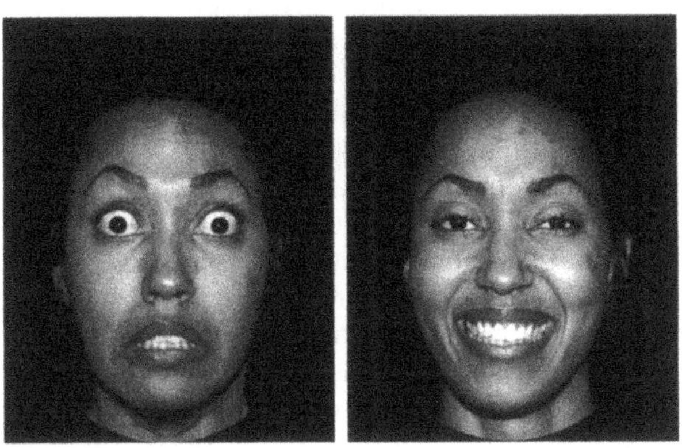

Figure 2. Stimuli used in Experiment 3.

orienting responses and the total fixation time (interrater reliability for 10% of the total participants, Cohen's kappa = .87 for the duration of fixation and .89 for the number of orientations).

Results and discussion

Preliminary statistical analyses showed no effects of order of presentation. As a consequence, data for each condition (happy vs fearful face) were collapsed across this factor. Two separate parametric tests were performed to compare the average total fixation time for each stimulus (fearful vs happy face) and the number of orientations in direction of each stimulus. Newborns showed significantly greater total looking time at the happy face ($M = 57$ s, $SD = 18.5$) than at the fearful face ($M = 46$ s, $SD = 8.8$), $t(11) = -2.8$, $p = .017$, but they did not orient more frequently to the happy face ($M = 21.5$, $SD = 8.7$) than to the fearful one ($M = 19.7$, $SD = 7.6$).

In contrast to the negative results found in the previous experiments, in Experiment 3 we obtained evidence for a significant preference to look for longer at a happy face than a fearful one.

GENERAL DISCUSSION

In Experiments 1 and 2 we found no evidence that newborns can discriminate, or prefer, a fearful expression as compared to a neutral expression. This is despite the fact that the fearful expression contains wide eyes and a semi-open mouth, features that may have enhanced the salience of a face. However, when we compared a fearful expression to a happy one, newborns looked significantly longer at the latter. This preference for a happy face also demonstrates that newborns are able to discriminate happy from fearful expressions. These results go beyond the previously contradictory evidence on newborns perception of facial expressions to show that at least some facial expressions are discriminated and preferred over others.

These results potentially inform two strands of theory about the early development of facial expression perception. One idea is that perception of facial expressions is acquired through experience, and the perceptual dimensions relevant to different expressions are gradually discovered and used to differentiate perceptual inputs and associate them with different responses and consequences (Quinn & Johnson, 1997). According to this general view it is not surprising that happy is preferred, even from the first few days, since this facial expression is likely to have been present for most of the time that face-related stimuli were present in the newborn's visual world. Early perceptual learning is therefore likely to acquire this expression first, and even possibly before a neutral expression. Effects of early experience on vocal expressions of emotion have already been described in newborns (Mastropieri & Turkewitz, 1999).

Another theoretical direction discussed earlier concerns cognitive neuroscience evidence for a rapid subcortical route sensitive to faces. In adults, this route is most sensitive to fearful expressions, possibly because of the wide eyes displayed in this expression (Whalen et al., 2004). One specific hypothesis is that this pathway may lead to aversion of fearful faces even in newborns. This prediction was not confirmed. Another hypothesis is that the subcortical route has a more general face detection role in infants and children (Johnson, 2005). This hypothesis is supported by functional MRI evidence that the amygdala is equally activated by neutral and fearful faces in children (Thomas et al., 2001). According to this hypothesis, fearful and neutral expressions both equally activate the subcortical route that may influence newborns face-related preferences (Johnson, 2005). Since these stimuli both activate the subcortical route they are both categorized as being the same kind of thing in the external world, and are therefore treated equivalently by the newborn. But, how are we to reconcile this view with the preference for a happy expression found in Experiment 3? It is important to note that while infants looked for significantly longer at the happy face as compared to the fearful one, they did not orient more frequently to this stimulus. Since orienting measures may better reflect the biases within a subcortical route (Johnson, 2005), a possibility is that the longer duration spent looking at the happy expression reflects experience acquired over the first few days. Orienting measures are likely to better reflect activity in subcortical pathways than fixation time since stimuli in the periphery impinge on the temporal visual field that is known to feed differentially into the subcortical visuo-motor route (de Gelder & Stekelenburg, 2005; Rafal, Henik, & Smith, 1992; Simion, Valenza, Umiltà, & Dalla Barba, 1995, 1998).

A further interpretation of our results relates to a recent study on the influence of the direction of the gaze on the perception of facial emotion in adults (Adams & Kleck, 2005). In this study it was demonstrated that when gaze direction matches the underlying behavioural intent (approach – avoidance) communicated by an emotional expression, the perception of that emotion would be enhanced. The authors demonstrated that direct gaze enhances the perception of approach-oriented emotions (anger and joy), while averted eye gaze enhances the perception of avoidance-oriented emotions (fear and sadness). According to this account, one possible interpretation of our results is that fearful faces are not preferred or discriminated by the newborns when associated with neutral faces because the direction of the gaze (i.e., direct gaze) is incongruent with the emotional expression communicated (i.e., fear). This hypothesis can be investigated in future work.

Whatever the mechanisms underlying the preference for happy expressions that we have observed, our results contribute to the growing body of evidence that, within the first few days after birth, newborns are sensitive to the characteristics of faces that are likely to maximize their chances of interacting with other conspecifics (Farroni et al., 2005).

REFERENCES

Adams, R. B., Jr., & Kleck, R. E. (2005). Effects of direct and averted gaze on the perception of facially communicated emotion. *Emotion, 5*, 3–11.

Adolphs, R., & Tranel, D. (2003). Amygdala damage impairs emotion recognition from scenes only when they contain facial expressions. *Neuropsychologia, 41*, 1281–1289.

Adolphs, R., Gosselin, F., Buchanan, T. W., Tranel, D., Schyns, P., & Damasio, A. R. (2005). A mechanism for impaired fear recognition after amygdala damage. *Nature, 433*, 22–23.

Darwin, C. (1872). *The expression of emotion in man and animals.* London: John Murray.

de Gelder, B. (2006). Towards the neurobiology of emotional body language. *Nature Reviews Neuroscience, 7*(3), 242–249.

de Gelder, B., & Stekelenburg, J. J. (2005). Nasal-temporal asymmetry of the N170 for processing faces in normal viewers but not in developmental prosopagnosia. *Neuroscience Letters, 376*, 40–45.

De Haan, M., & Nelson, C. A. (1998). Discrimination and categorization of facial expressions of emotion during infancy. In A. Slater (Ed.), *Perceptual development* (pp. 287–309). Hove, UK: Psychology Press.

Ekman, P., Friesen, W. V., & Ellworth, P. (1972). *Emotion in the human face.* New York: Pergamon Press.

Farroni, T., Csibra, G., Simion, F., & Johnson, M. H. (2002). Eye contact detection in humans from birth. *Proceedings of the National Academy of Sciences (PNAS), 99*, 9602–9605.

Farroni, T., Johnson, M. H., Menon, E., Zulian, L., Faraguna, D., & Csibra, G. (2005). Newborns' preference for face-relevant stimuli: Effect of contrast polarity. *Proceeding of the National Academy of Sciences (PNAS), 102*, 17245–17250.

Field, T., Woodson, R., Greenberg, R., & Cohen, D. (1982). Discrimination and imitation of facial expression by neonates. *Science, 218*, 179–181.

Field, T. M., Woodson, R., Greenberg, R., & Cohen, D. (1983). Discrimination and imitation of facial expressions by neonates. *Annual Progress in Child Psychiatry & Child Development, 16*, 119–125.

Johnson, M. H. (2005). Subcortical face processing. *Nature Reviews Neuroscience, 6*, 766–774.

Johnson, M. H., Dziurawiec, S., Ellis, H., & Morton, J. (1991). Newborns' preferential tracking of face-like stimuli and its subsequent decline. *Cognition, 40*, 1–19.

Kaitz, M., Meschulach-Sarfaty, O., Auerbach, J., & Eidelman, A. (1988). A re-examination of newborns' ability to imitate facial expressions. *Developmental Psychology, 24*, 3–7.

Kotsoni, E., De Haan, M., & Johnson, M. H. (2001). Categorical perception of facial expressions by 7-month-old infants. *Perception, 30*, 1115–1125.

Mastropieri, D., & Turkewitz, G. (1999). Prenatal experience and neonatal responsiveness to vocal expressions of emotion. *Developmental Psychobiology, 35*, 204–214.

Nelson, C. A., & Dolgin, K. (1985). The generalized discrimination of facial expressions by 7-month-old infants. *Child Development, 56*, 58–61.

Pascalis, O., & de Schonen, S. (1994). Recognition memory in 3- to 4-day-old human neonates. *Neuroreport, 5*, 1721–1724.

Pascalis, O., de Schonen, S., Morton, J., Deruelle, C., & Fabre-Grenet, M. (1995). Mother's face recognition by neonates: A replication and an extension. *Infant Behavior and Development*, *18*, 79–85.

Quinn, P. C., & Johnson, M. H. (1997). The emergence of category representations in infants: A connectionist analysis. *Journal of Experimental Child Psychology*, *66*, 236–263.

Rafal, R., Henik, A., & Smith, J. (1992). Extrageniculate contributions to reflex visual orienting in normal humans a temporal hemifield advantage. *Journal of Cognitive Neuroscience*, *3*, 323–329.

Simion, F., Valenza, E., Umiltà, C., & Dalla Barba, B. (1995). Inhibition of return in newborns is temporo-nasal asymmetrical. *Infant Behavior and Development*, *18*, 189–194.

Simion, F., Valenza, E., Umiltà, C., & Dalla Barba, B. (1998). Preferential orienting to faces in newborns: A temporal-nasal asymmetry. *Journal of Experimental Psychology: Human Perception and Performance*, *24*, 1399–1405.

Slater, A., Morison, V., Town, C., & Rose, D. (1985). Movement perception and identity constancy in the new-born infant. *British Journal of Developmental Psychology*, *3*, 211–220.

Thomas, K. M., Drevets, W. C., Whalen, P. J., Eccard, C. H., Dahl, R. E., Ryan, N. D., et al. (2001). Amygdala responses to facial expressions in children and adults. *Biological Psychiatry*, *49*, 309–316.

Valenza, E., Simion, F., Macchi Cassia, V., & Umiltà, C. (1996). Face preference at birth. *Journal of experimental psychology: Human Perception and Performance*, *22*, 892–903.

Whalen, P. J., Kagan, J., Cook, R. G., Davis, F. C., Kim, H., Polis, S. et al. (2004). Human amygdala responsivity to masked fearful eye whites. *Science*, *306*, 2061.

EUROPEAN JOURNAL OF DEVELOPMENTAL PSYCHOLOGY
2007, 4 (1), 14–30

Imitation of intentional actions and internal state language in infancy predict preschool theory of mind skills

Kara M. Olineck and Diane Poulin-Dubois
Concordia University, Montréal, Québec, Canada

The present study examined whether infants' imitation of intentional actions, concurrent vocabulary, and later internal state lexicon predicted their "theory of mind" (ToM) at preschool age. Initially, 14- and 18-month-olds completed an imitation task on intentional action understanding. Concurrent general vocabulary and internal state language at 32 months was also assessed. At approximately 4 years of age, children were retested with an interactive game measuring intention understanding, a false belief task or the Theory of Mind Scale (Wellman & Liu, 2004), and the PPVT. Infants' performance on the imitation task predicted their later concept of intention. Furthermore, internal state language was highly predictive of later ToM. These findings suggest that there is developmental continuity between precursors to ToM in infancy and ToM in the preschool years.

Adults are constantly making inferences about the mental states underlying human behaviour, a process that is called "theory of mind" (ToM). We see people as having mental states, such as beliefs about the world and desires for objects, and we understand their behaviour based on this knowledge.

Correspondence should be addressed to Diane Poulin-Dubois, Department of Psychology, PY-170, Concordia University, 7141 Sherbrooke Street West, Montréal, Québec, Canada, H4B 1R6. E-mail: diane.poulindubois@concordia.ca

This research was supported by an operating grant awarded to the second author from the Social Sciences and Humanities Research Council of Canada. The first author was supported by a graduate fellowship from the Natural Sciences and Engineering Research Council of Canada (NSERC). This research was submitted by Kara M. Olineck in partial fulfillment of the requirements for the doctoral degree in psychology at Concordia University. Portions of this work were presented in June 2006 at the XVth Biennial International Conference on Infant Studies, Kyoto, Japan.

The authors wish to thank Lauren Gilbert, Sandra Misrachi, and Sara Quirke for help with collecting and coding the data.

DOI: 10.1080/17405620601046931

Research has demonstrated that by the time children reach 4 or 5 years of age, they have a similar understanding of people as psychological beings (Wellman, Cross, & Watson, 2001). However, much less is known about the putative precursors of ToM in infancy. A common criticism of experiments investigating the origins of ToM in infancy is that it is unclear whether the tasks that have been designed to tap into infants' early concept of the mind are actually measuring what they are intended to measure. For instance, some researchers have argued that infants' ability to predict how a person will act could be based simply on learned rules about behaviour rather than on a conception that the mind mediates behaviour (Perner & Ruffman, 2005). One way of establishing the external validity of these tasks is to determine whether there is continuity between children's early social-cognitive abilities and their later, more advanced, ToM skills. To date, there are very few longitudinal studies that have addressed this important gap in the literature. Therefore, the main goal of the present investigation was to systematically examine the continuity between children's performance on ToM tasks in infancy and the preschool period.

An active line of work has focused on infants' understanding of intentionality as the first step in developing a full-fledged ToM. Intention can be used to denote deliberate action as opposed to accidental action and to refer to the reason why something is done (Astington, 2001). By the end of the first year, infants are learning to identify the intentions underlying other people's behaviour. Specifically, they are sensitive to goal-directed actions and can detect the goals of other people using cues such as eye gaze, reaching, and emotional expressions (Baird & Baldwin, 2001; Phillips, Wellman, & Spelke, 2002; Woodward, 1998, 2003). During the second year of life, research has indicated that infants display a more advanced understanding of intention (e.g., Bellagamba & Tomasello, 1999; Meltzoff, 1995). For instance, in an investigation that aimed to uncover infants' implicit understanding of intention, Carpenter, Akhtar, and Tomasello (1998) modelled intentional and accidental actions to infants ranging from 14 to 18 months of age, and measured whether they preferred to imitate those actions that were completed intentionally. Overall, they found that, regardless of age, infants reproduced significantly more intentional than accidental actions. However, the limited number of infants at either end of their age range might have prevented them from detecting a developmental progression in infants' conception of intention. In order to more systematically investigate this issue, Olineck and Poulin-Dubois (2005) recently replicated and extended these findings by testing separate groups of 14- and 18-month-old infants. Importantly, the results revealed a developmental progression in infants' ability to differentiate intentional from accidental actions between 14 and 18 months of age. Taken together, these empirical studies suggest that infants understand intentional actions early on.

Additional evidence for an implicit understanding of intention and other mental states has been documented in children's early use of internal state terms during their everyday conversations (e.g., Bartsch & Wellman, 1995; Bretherton & Beeghly, 1982; Shatz, Wellman, & Silber, 1983). For instance, in a longitudinal study of 10 children who were followed from 1 to 6 years of age, Bartsch and Wellman (1995) found that children's conversations about the mind begin early with talk about desires and intentions (e.g., want, wish). Recently, an active line of research in ToM development has been focusing on the role that language might play in bringing the child from an implicit to an explicit understanding of the mind. Although there is no consensus about what aspect of language is involved in ToM development, it is well established that linguistic ability predicts performance on tests of ToM (Astington & Baird, 2005). For instance, it has been shown that individuals suffering from language deficits also tend to display delayed ToM development (Baron-Cohen, Baldwin, & Crowson, 1997; Bloom, 2000; Garfield, Peterson, & Perry, 2001; Tager-Flusberg, 1992). In addition, longitudinal research on language and ToM indicates that individual differences in language competence explain later individual variability in ToM skill between the ages of 2 and 3 years (e.g., Astington & Jenkins, 1999; Brown, Donelan-McCall, & Dunn, 1996; Ruffman, Slade, & Crowe, 2002; Watson, Painter, & Bornstein, 2002). Taken together, these and other investigations provide empirical evidence to suggest that language is an important antecedent to ToM development.

What remains to be investigated is whether there is continuity between children's implicit ToM in infancy, their use of internal state terms, and their explicit concept of people as mentalists in the preschool period. Many theoretical accounts propose that infants' social-cognitive abilities are related to later ToM ability. For example, it has been suggested that the emergence of joint attention skills in the second year of life is evidence for infants' understanding of intentional behaviour (Baron-Cohen, 1995; Camaioni, 1992, 1997; Tomasello, 1995). Other researchers have proposed that imitation, which reflects the understanding of a match between oneself and the other, is the bedrock of ToM development (Meltzoff & Gopnik, 1993; Rogers & Pennington, 1991). Finally, pretend play has been proposed as an early manifestation of children's capacity for meta-representation (Leslie, 1987, 1994).

Despite much theorizing about the continuity of ToM in infancy and the preschool years, there is surprisingly little direct empirical evidence to support the theoretical positions just reviewed. In fact, only a handful of longitudinal studies have investigated the hypothesis of a developmental continuity in ToM development from infancy to childhood. In one of the first studies, Youngblade and Dunn (1995) investigated whether there were links between infants' pretend play with peers at 33 months of age and their ability to understand other people's feelings and pass standard false belief tasks at 40 months of age. Importantly, they found that children who engaged in more pretend play when they were 33 months old were better at identifying feelings and recognizing false-beliefs 7 months later. Another longitudinal study examining the continuity of ToM skills was conducted by Charman et al. (2000). These researchers initially measured 20-month-old play, joint attention, and imitation skills. Then, when these children were 44 months of age, they completed a battery of ToM tasks, including a standard false belief measure. Interestingly, joint attention behaviours, but not imitation or play, were associated with ToM ability at 44 months. More recently, Wellman, Phillips, Dunphy-Lelii, and LaLonde (2004) found that there was continuity between infants' understanding of goal-directed actions at 14 months, as measured with an infant-controlled habituation procedure, and their general concept of the mind at 4 years of age. Most recently, Olineck and Poulin-Dubois (2005) conducted the first longitudinal study to examine the link between infants' ability to distinguish intentional and accidental actions and their later production of internal state language. Fourteen- and eighteen-month-olds were administered an imitation task (adapted from Carpenter et al., 1998) in which an experimenter modelled accidental and intentional actions using toy devices. Then, when these children reached 32 months, their parents completed a 78-item questionnaire on their children's internal state language production, which was based on Bretherton and Beeghly (1982). The main findings revealed that infants who were more likely to only imitate an intentional action had a larger internal state lexicon at 32 months. Taken together, these results and those of the other few studies conducted recently are consistent with the hypothesis of continuity between early social-cognitive skills and later ToM. However, the specificity of the link between implicit and explicit ToM skills, as well as the factors that can account for this important developmental transition, remain to be examined.

The goal of the present study was to systematically investigate the relationship between children's understanding of intention-in-action and general language skills in infancy, internal state language in toddlerhood, and ToM in the preschool period. Specifically, we examined the potential links between early nonverbal and mature forms of intention understanding. Intention understanding is particularly central to social competence because understanding others' intentions is necessary in many interactive contexts (Tomasello, Carpenter, Call, Behne, & Moll, 2005). We also examined to what extent general verbal skills and mental state vocabulary in infancy can predict general ToM development years later. In the present experiment, children who originally participated in an imitation task when they were 14 or 18 months old and whose parents provided information regarding their internal state language at 32 months were invited to return to the laboratory when they were approximately 50 months of age. During this second laboratory visit, participants completed three tasks: (1) a target-hitting game adapted from Phillips, Baron-Cohen, and Rutter (1998), which was designed to measure preschool children's ability to answer questions about their own intentions; (2) a standard "unexpected contents" false belief task or the Theory of Mind Scale (Wellman & Liu, 2004); and (3) the Peabody Picture Vocabulary Test (PPVT; Dunn & Dunn, 1997), which measures receptive vocabulary by asking children to point to a picture that corresponds with a word. We expected that there would be a significant relationship between children's implicit concept of intention measured during infancy and their more explicit understanding of intention during the preschool years. In addition, we hypothesized that children's performance on the action imitation task at 14–18 months would be related to their later concept of the mind, as measured by the false belief task and the Theory of Mind Scale. Finally, we predicted that there would be continuity between children's general language skills between 14 and 18 months, their use of internal state at 32 months of age, and their performance on preschool ToM tasks at 50 months of age.

METHOD

Participants

Twenty-six 14-month-olds and 30 18-month-olds participated in an action imitation task, and their parents completed the MacArthur Short Form Vocabulary Checklist: Level II Form A (MCDI; Fenson et al., 2000). Approximately three years later, 15 of the children initially tested at 14 months and 16 of the children initially tested at 18 months returned to the laboratory to participate in the present follow-up experiment (20 females and 11 males; $M = 50.05$ months, $SD = 4.37$, range = 45.26–55.43 months). Parents of 26 of these children also completed a questionnaire regarding their children's internal state language production at 32 months of age ($M = 31.99$, $SD = 0.43$, range = 31.03–33.13 months).

Materials

Imitation task. A rectangular wooden box (38 cm long, 25 cm wide, 9 cm tall) with six removable lids was constructed. Embedded in the centre of each of the box lids were toy devices that could be easily manipulated by the infant (e.g., handle that twists). Two of the box lids were always used in the warm-up phase of testing, and the remaining four lids were randomly assigned to four experimental trials. One of the lids used in the warm-up phase of testing included one toy device, and the remaining five box lids included two toy devices that were matched for size and level of attractiveness. The base of the box was visibly connected to a computer monitor via a telephone cord. Following the action demonstration, computer animations were surreptitiously activated by the experimenter and were displayed on the monitor.

Target-hitting game. A wooden structure (approximately 10 cm wide and 40 cm high), which shelved 6 different coloured plastic canisters, was constructed. These plastic containers (7 cm wide and 7 cm tall) served as the targets for the game. They were easy to open and had the capacity to hold small prizes (e.g., ball, stickers). Half of the canisters contained a prize and half of them were empty. The plastic canisters were placed on a platform that consisted of six holes large enough to allow them to drop through when activated. The cans rested on small metal rods that were retracted electronically with a universal remote control (i.e., magic wand). Children were told that the objective of the game was to hit the cans off the wall by aiming the "magic wand" at a predetermined target. Indeed, the manipulation of the remote appeared to cause the can that was hit to fall from the wall directly. However, a hidden experimenter specified which canister fell off the shelf using a hand-held toggle switch with six positions corresponding to the six locations on the shelf. Therefore, the participant was in control of when the canister fell, but the hidden experimenter determined which canister fell. A flipbook representing the target colour for each trial served as a visual reminder of the canister the child was intending to hit for each trial.

False belief task. The props used in this task included a female puppet, an empty Smarties box, and 4 crayons.

Theory of Mind Scale. Brief vignettes adapted from Wellman and Liu (2004) were used, as well as toy figurines, puppets, pictures, and a Smarties box containing crayons. Children's responses during this and the above tasks were videotaped.

Peabody Picture Vocabulary Test (PPVT; Dunn & Dunn, 1997). In order to administer this standardized language measure, the following were used: the test manual, the test book containing a series of pictures, and the standard response forms.

Procedure and design

Imitation task. The procedure was adapted from Carpenter and her colleagues (1998) and is described in detail in Olineck and Poulin-Dubois

(2005). After two warm-up trials designed to familiarize infants with the imitation task, infants were shown demonstrations in which the investigator modelled a sequence of two actions, using the toy devices. One of the actions was portrayed as accidental and the other as intentional. The accidental action consisted of the investigator looking away from the box lid, while completing the action, and then putting a hand to her mouth and saying, "Whoops!" with suitable intonation. Additionally, during the "accident" the investigator's face registered surprise and her upper body jumped up slightly. The intentional action consisted of the investigator looking attentively at one of the specific devices, completing the action slowly, and then smiling and saying, "There," with appropriate intonation. During the completion of the intentional action, the investigator also leaned slightly toward the devices. The action sequence demonstrated by the investigator always resulted in activating a computer animation display. Then, the infants were given the opportunity to activate the computer animation. It was activated approximately two seconds after infants reproduced the intentional action. This delay provided infants with the opportunity to also reproduce the accidental action. The computer animation was not activated in cases where infants only reproduced the accidental action. If infants failed to activate the end result, the investigator proceeded to the next experimental trial. During the test phase, the order of the action sequence (i.e., accidental–intentional or intentional–accidental) alternated across the four trials. In addition, the side of the intentional action was counterbalanced, as well as the order in which the four experimental box lids were presented.

Target-hitting game. The procedure for this task was modelled after Phillips et al. (1998). Children were told that the objective of the game was to use a magic wand to hit the canisters on the wall and win some prizes. They were informed that some of the cans contained a prize and some of them were empty. Following a brief demonstration by the experimenter, a warm-up phase consisting of two trials was administered. In both warm-up trials, the child always hit the target can; however, they only won one prize. During the test phase, the same procedure was employed. After the child hit a can and removed the lid to see if they had won a prize, the experimenter responded with either, "Oh look, you won a prize!" or "Oh look, no prize this time." The child was asked to hold the open canister (which either contained or did not contain a prize depending on the trial) in their hands while the experimenter said, "Listen carefully. Which can did you try to hit? The [insert colour] or the [insert colour]?" For half the trials, the colour that was mentioned first was the target and the colour mentioned second was one of the cans directly beside the target. For the remaining trials, the target colour was mentioned second.

The task consisted of a combination of hit (H), miss (M), prize (P), and no prize (NP) outcomes. A hit was achieved when the target can fell off the wall, and a miss occurred when the can beside the target fell down instead. Regardless of whether the trial was set up to be a hit or a miss, a can always fell off the wall. In order to isolate intention understanding from the desire to win a prize, there were two discrepant conditions in which the child either missed the target but won a prize (MP) or hit the intended can but did not win a prize (HNP). There were also two consistent conditions that could be answered based on desire and/or intention understanding: trials in which a prize was awarded when the target was hit (HP) or not awarded when a miss occurred (MNP). A total of 16 trials were administered, with 4 trials per condition. The condition (i.e., hit and miss) and outcome (i.e., prize and no prize) of the trials were counterbalanced. In addition, the order was arranged in a quasi-random fashion so that no outcome (i.e., prize vs no prize), condition (i.e., hit vs miss), or target colour appeared more than twice in a row. Children's responses to the test question were recorded, and the number of times they correctly identified the intended target was coded (maximum = 16).

False belief task. Children were shown a Smarties box and asked what they thought the box contained. If they did not spontaneously respond "candies" or "chocolates" the experimenter prompted them by pointing to the pictures on the box. After they responded correctly, the experimenter opened the box and revealed that there were really crayons inside. Then the experimenter put the crayons back inside the box, and asked the child what was really inside the Smarties box. Next, the experimenter introduced a puppet and asked the children what Dora thought was in the box and whether she saw inside the box. Children were coded as having passed the false belief task if they told the experimenter that Dora thought there were Smarties in the box and that she had not seen inside the box.

Theory of Mind Scale. Children were presented with five interactive stories (see Wellman & Liu, 2004, for detailed descriptions), using toy figurines, pictures, and/or puppets, and were then asked questions regarding their own mental states and those of the story characters. The stories tapped into children's knowledge of other people's desires, beliefs, knowledge access, false beliefs, and the contrast between real and apparent emotions. The experimenter coded whether children responded correctly to the questions measuring their understanding of the five mental states, and assigned children a total score (maximum = 5) on the Theory of Mind Scale. The criteria provided by Wellman and Liu (2004) were utilized when evaluating children's responses to the test questions. In addition to their overall score on the scale, children's performance on the false belief task (i.e., pass or fail) was coded separately. Wellman and Liu (2004) consistently presented the story about diverse desires in the first or second position and the story regarding real and apparent emotions in the fourth or fifth positions. In the present experiment, the diverse desires task was always presented first and the real – apparent emotion task was always presented last. The remaining stories were presented in counterbalanced order, which results in a total of six orders for the tasks comprising the Theory of Mind Scale.

Peabody Picture Vocabulary Test (PPVT; Dunn & Dunn, 1997). The standardized protocol was used. Children's responses were recorded during the administration of the test, and they were assigned a standard score.

The children initially tested at 14 months completed the target-shooting game, the PPVT, and the false belief task. When the 18-month-olds returned to the lab, we had access to the Theory of Mind Scale (Wellman & Liu, 2004), and therefore these children completed this measure, which includes the false belief task. All children completed the target-shooting game first; however the order of the PPVT and the false belief task/Theory of Mind Scale were counterbalanced across participants.

Reliability

In order to establish interrater reliability, 20% of the data ($n = 6$) was coded by a second coder. There was 100% agreement between the coders across the three tasks.

RESULTS

The first question of interest was whether there was continuity between children's performance on the action imitation task at 14 – 18 months and their performance on the target-shooting game at 50 months. To represent children's performance on the imitation task in infancy, we utilized two dependent variables: (1) the difference between the percentage of time children reproduced the intentional action (out of 4) and the percentage of time they imitated the accidental action (out of 4) (i.e., Difference Score = % intentional actions imitated – % of accidental actions completed) ($M = 25.81$, $SD = 21.87$, range = 0 – 50), and (2) the percentage of time they imitated the intentional action first ($M = 55.65$, $SD = 25.58$, range = 0 – 100). The performance of the children included in the present longitudinal sample ($N = 31$) was comparable to that of those who did not participate ($N = 25$) for each of these two variables. To represent children's performance on the target-shooting game, two dependent variables were also used. We computed children's score in each of the discrepant conditions: (1) when children hit the target but did not win a prize (HNP: $M = 3.68$, $SD = 0.87$, range = 0 – 4), and (2) when children missed the target but won a prize

(MP: $M = 1.35$, $SD = 1.52$, range = 0–4). We analyzed children's performance in these two specific conditions because their intention (i.e., to hit a predetermined target) was distinct from their desire (i.e., to win a prize). In the original study by Phillips et al. (1998), children's performance on trials where the mental state of intention was isolated revealed a developmental shift in their concept of intention between 4 and 5 years of age. To examine whether there was a link between children's performance on intention tasks in infancy and the preschool years, we computed Pearson correlations between all of these dependent variables. We found a significant positive correlation between the percentage of time children imitated the intentional action first and their score in the HNP condition of the preschool task, $r = .50$, $p < .01$. No other correlations reached statistical significance.

Our second question of interest was whether there was continuity between children's performance on the action imitation task at 14–18 months and their more general concept of the mind during preschool years, as measured by their performance on either the standard false belief task or the Theory of Mind Scale. All of the children who participated in the present study completed the false belief task. Ten of the children passed this task and 21 of them failed. Point biserial correlations were computed with the two dependent variables reflecting children's performance on the action imitation task in infancy. No statistically significant relationships were found. As outlined earlier, the children initially tested at 18 months ($n = 16$) completed the Theory of Mind Scale. It was noted that their total scores on the Theory of Mind Scale ($M = 2.88$, $SD = 1.36$, range = 0–5) were comparable to those obtained by children ranging from 50–53 months of age in another recent study ($M = 2.9$, range = 0–5; Wellman & Liu, 2004). Because children's performance on the false belief task was coded separately, the dependent variable used for the present study was children's score on the other four tasks comprising the Theory of Mind Scale ($M = 2.56$, $SD = 1.09$, range = 0–4). Pearson correlations were computed between this score and the dependent variables characterizing the imitation task. No significant relationships were found.

Next, we examined whether children's performance across the three preschool tasks was related. First, Pearson correlations were computed between children's score on the PPVT ($M = 100.03$, $SD = 13.95$, range = 56–129) and the two dependent variables reflecting their performance on the target-hitting game. No significant correlations were found. Second, we ran a point biserial correlation between children's performance on the false belief task and their scores on the PPVT. Not surprisingly, we found that children with better general language skills were also more likely to pass the false belief task ($r_{pbi} = .48$, $p < .05$). We also ran a Pearson correlation between children's PPVT and their score on the Theory of Mind Scale and found no significant relation. Furthermore, to examine the coherence between preschoolers' concept of intention and their knowledge of other mental states, we computed point biserial correlations between children's performance on the false belief task and their scores on the two dependent variables reflecting their performance on the target-hitting game. No significant correlations were found. We also ran Pearson correlations between their scores on the Theory of Mind Scale (excluding the false belief task) and their scores on the two dependent variables characterizing the target-hitting game ($n = 16$). Again, no significant correlations were found. Finally, we ran a point biserial correlation between children's performance on the false belief task and the other four tasks comprising the Theory of Mind Scale. As expected, we found that children who passed the false belief task also performed better on the Theory of Mind Scale ($r_{pbi} = .65$, $p < .05$).

In the next series of analyses, we examined whether there was continuity between children's general language skills between 14 and 18 months and their performance on ToM tasks at 4 years of age. First, we ran Pearson correlations between children's total score on the MCDI at 14–18 months and the dependent variables characterizing their performance on the target-hitting game at 50 months. No statistically significant correlations emerged. Next, we computed a point biserial correlation between children's total scores on the MCDI at 14–18 months and their performance on the standard false belief task at 50 months. Interestingly, we found that children who scored higher on the MCDI in infancy were also more likely to pass the false belief task at 50 months ($r_{pbi} = .45$, $p < .05$). We also correlated children's total scores on the MCDI at 14–18 months and their performance on the Theory of mind Scale, excluding the false belief task. This relationship was not significant.

Our final question of interest was whether there is continuity between children's use of internal state terms at 32 months and their performance on ToM tasks at 50 months. As described earlier, parents of 26 of the children who participated in this follow-up investigation also provided data regarding their child's internal state language at 32 months of age. In this subset of children, there continued to be sufficient variability in their internal state language production ($M = 47.35$, $SD = 18.34$, range $= 10–72$). We computed Pearson correlations between children's internal state language and their performance on the target-hitting game according to the two dependent variables outlined previously. No statistically significant correlations emerged. Next, we computed a point biserial correlation between their performance on the false belief task and their previous internal state language production. The results indicated that children who passed the false belief task at approximately 50 months also produced more internal state terms at 32 months of age ($r_{pbi} = .43$, $p < .05$). Finally, we computed a Pearson correlation between children's score on the other four tasks comprising the Theory of Mind Scale, and their previous internal state language production. Once again, we found a predictive relationship ($r = .55$, $p < .05$). In order to account for the effect of language, a partial correlation controlling for children's score on the PPVT, was computed. This correlation was marginally significant, indicating that children's use of internal state language at 32 months predicts their performance on the Theory of Mind Scale, even when general language abilities are accounted for ($r = .51$, $p = .07$). All correlations computed between children's performance on the infant imitation task, internal state language, and preschool theory of mind tasks are represented in Table 1.

To summarize, the present study revealed a significant positive relationship between children's ability to differentiate between intentional and accidental actions in infancy and their later, more advanced, concept of intention in the preschool years. Specifically, we found that children who were more likely to reproduce the intentional action before the accidental action during the infant imitation task were also more likely to perform better on the target-hitting game. To our knowledge, this is the first study to provide preliminary evidence for a long-term association between children's implicit and explicit understanding of intention, from infancy to the preschool years. As expected, we also found a significant predictive relationship between infants' general vocabulary in the second year (i.e., MCDI scores) and their later performance on the false belief task. Moreover, consistent with findings from other laboratories (e.g., Wellman et al., 2004), we found a significant link between children's scores on the PPVT and their performance on the false belief task. An interesting finding from this research was that children's use of internal state language at 32 months predicted their performance on the false belief task. Furthermore, children who produced more internal state terms at 32 months also scored higher on the other four tasks comprising the Theory of Mind Scale. Importantly, this predictive relationship was not uniquely language driven,

TABLE 1
Intercorrelations between children's performance on infant imitation task, internal state language, and their performance on preschool theory of mind tasks

	HNP	*MP*	*FB*	*ToM Scale (n = 16)*
Infant task: Intentional action first	.50**	−.18	.05	−.02
Infant task: Difference score	.19	−.01	−.10	−.07
MCDI score (14–18 months)	.02	−.16	.45*	.42
Internal state language at 32 months ($n = 26$)	−.14	.06	.43*	.55*
Target-hitting game: HNP score (HNP)		−.26	−.16	−.19
Target-hitting game: MP score (MP)			−.04	.00
False belief task (FB).				65*

Note: $^{**}p < .01$; $^{*}p < .05$.

as the correlation remained marginally significant when general language abilities were accounted for. These findings provide further evidence to suggest that there is a long-term association between children's early talk about the mind and their later ToM skills.

DISCUSSION

Despite the fact that there is much speculation about the foundations of ToM in infancy, there has been little empirical evidence to support the claims that early social-cognitive abilities are precursors to a ToM. Only a handful of studies have examined the developmental continuity in precursors of ToM concepts such as desire, intention, and attention. In a recent paper, Wellman et al. (2004) reported a correlation between 14-month-old infants' attention decrement in a task measuring goal-directed action and their later ToM skills. However, these findings might simply reflect a general developmental status similar to the well-known relationship between attention decrement and later IQ (McCall & Carriger, 1993). The present study is the first to show that there may be relationships between children's early forms of intention understanding in infancy, their use of internal state language, and their more advanced understanding of the concept of intention at preschool age.

More specifically, the results of this experiment suggest that there is a link between children's ability to differentiate between intentional and accidental actions in infancy and their later, more advanced, concept of intention in the preschool years. In particular, we found that children who were more likely to reproduce the intentional action first during the imitation task also performed better on the preschool intention task. The other dependent variable reflecting infants' imitation of intentional actions did not correlate with preschool measures. This is likely due to the fact that that this dependent measure had reduced variability. Interestingly, the outcome variable from the preschool intention task that yielded positive findings is the critical condition, that is, the one that requires understanding of intention as distinct from desire. The present study provides preliminary evidence to suggest that there is developmental continuity between children's understanding of intention-in-action in infancy and their later, more advanced, understanding of intention in the mind. The fact that a long-term longitudinal association was observed between tasks that measure the same construct (i.e., intention) is an important finding. This data is consistent with a theoretical account that emphasizes infants' early sensitivity to the intentional structure of people's actions as playing a key role in children's developing understanding of people as mentalists. This seems to contrast with one previous longitudinal study that reported no association between imitation skills at 20 months and a battery of ToM abilities at 44 months (Charman et al., 2000). However, rather than testing general imitation skills per se, the task that we administered at 14 and 18 months tapped into infants' ability to differentiate intentional from accidental actions, using a range of behaviour cues such as gaze, gestures, and vocalizations. As such, the present imitation tasks probably required good joint attention skills, which are themselves predictive of concurrent imitation of intentional actions and later ToM (Camaioni, Perucchini, Bellagamba, & Colonnesi, 2004; Charman et al., 2000). Thus, infants' ability to monitor and imitate the goals or intentions underlying other people's actions might be one of the critical steps towards developing a full-fledged concept of intention. Unexpectedly, we did not find that children's performance on the imitation task in infancy was related to their later understanding of false belief or other mental states (e.g., desire, knowledge, emotion). As such, it is necessary for future research to examine whether a battery of infancy tasks tapping into a wide range of mental states would predict performance on the Theory of Mind Scale at preschool age. To our knowledge, the present investigation included the largest sample of children ever tested in a longitudinal study examining ToM from infancy to the preschool years. Nevertheless, it is possible that more significant relationships between concepts in infancy and the preschool age may have been detected with a larger sample size. This limitation should also be addressed in future longitudinal investigations.

Another important finding of the present study is that internal state language is highly predictive of later ToM. Specifically, we found that there was a significant relationship between children's use of internal state terms at 32 months and their general concept of the mind at 50 months, as measured by the false belief task. There was also a significant positive correlation between children's internal state term production at 32 months and their performance on the other four tasks comprising the Theory of Mind Scale, even when general language skills (i.e., PPVT) were partialled out. By demonstrating that children's internal state language is highly predictive of ToM skills approximately two years later, this study extends previous research that has shown a similar link during the preschool period (Brown et al., 1996; Ruffman et al., 2002). Moreover, the strong link that we observed between the number of internal terms produced by children at 32 months and their performance on ToM tasks at 4.5 years supports the hypothesis that talking about mental states helps children learn about the mind (Hugues & Dunn, 1998; Ruffman et al., 2002). With respect to ToM and general language skills, the present study also went beyond previous research in uncovering a significant predictive link between general language and ToM over the largest developmental span ever studied, that is, between 14 and 54 months. We found a significant correlation between children's scores on the PPVT and their performance on the false belief task, which replicates previous research (Astington & Baird, 2005). In contrast, we did not find that children's scores on the PPVT were significantly related to their performance on the other four tasks that comprise the Theory of Mind Scale. These results replicate the findings recently reported by Wellman et al. (2004), who also demonstrated that the Theory of Mind Scale is a less language-laden measure of ToM.

In conclusion, the data of the present study are consistent with the hypothesis that there is continuity in social cognition between infancy and early childhood. This longitudinal study cannot answer questions about the mechanism by which precursors, such as the ones we have uncovered, affect later abilities. However, our demonstration of developmental continuities in the realm of social cognition provides critical information with regards to the controversy about the nature of early social-cognitive abilities (see Perner & Ruffman, 2005, for a lean interpretation of nonverbal tasks of mind reading skills). We believe that the results of the present investigation provide preliminary evidence to support the hypothesis that imitation of intentional actions and internal state language production tap into infants' early concept of the mind. Regardless of whether these precursors reflect infants' ability to acquire sophisticated behavioural rules or an implicit ToM, the present findings indicate that these abilities are somehow related to the acquisition of a full-fledged ToM.

REFERENCES

Astington, J. W. (2001). The paradox of intention: Assessing children's metarepresentational understanding. In B. F. Malle, L. J. Moses, & D. A. Baldwin (Eds.), *Intentions and intentionality: Foundations of social cognition* (pp. 85–103). Cambridge, MA: MIT Press.

Astington, J. W., & Baird, J. A. (Eds.). (2005). *Why language matters for theory of mind.* New York: Oxford University Press.

Astington, J. W., & Jenkins, J. M. (1999). A longitudinal study of the relation between language and theory-of-mind development. *Developmental Psychology, 35*, 1311–1320.

Baird, J. A., & Baldwin, D. A. (2001). Making sense of human behavior: Action parsing and intentional inference. In B. F. Malle, L. J. Moses, & D. A. Baldwin (Eds.), *Intentions and intentionality: Foundations of social cognition* (pp. 193–206). Cambridge, MA: MIT Press.

Baron-Cohen, S. (1995). *Mindblindness: An essay on autism and theory of mind.* Cambridge, MA: MIT Press.

Baron-Cohen, S., Baldwin, D. A., & Crowson, M. (1997). Do children with autism use the speaker's direction of gaze strategy to crack the code of language? *Child Development, 68*, 48–57.

Bartsch, K., & Wellman, H. M. (1995). *Children talk about the mind.* New York: Oxford University Press.

Bellagamba, F., & Tomasello, M. (1999). Re-enacting intended acts: Comparing 12- and 18-month-olds. *Infant Behavior and Development, 22*, 277–282.

Bloom, P. (2000). *How children learn the meanings of words.* Cambridge, MA: MIT Press.

Bretherton, I., & Beeghly, M. (1982). Talking about internal states: The acquisition of an explicit theory of mind. *Developmental Psychology, 18*, 906–921.

Brown, J. R., Donelan-McCall, N., & Dunn, J. (1996). Why talk about mental states? The significance of children's conversations with friends, siblings, and mothers. *Child Development*, *67*, 836–849.

Camaioni, L. (1992). Mind knowledge in infancy. The emergence of intentional communication. *Early Development and Parenting*, *1*, 15–22.

Camaioni, L. (1997). The emergence of intentional communication in ontogeny, phylogeny and pathology. *European Psychologist*, *2*, 216–225.

Camaioni, L., Perucchini, P., Bellagamba, F., & Colonnesi, C. (2004). The role of declarative pointing in developing a theory of mind. *Infancy*, *5*, 291–308.

Carpenter, M., Akhtar, N., & Tomasello, M. (1998). Fourteen- through 18-month-old infants differentially imitate intentional and accidental actions. *Infant Behavior & Development*, *21*, 315–330.

Charman, T., Baron-Cohen, S., Swettenham, J., Baird, G., Cox, A., & Drew, A. (2000). Testing joint attention, imitation, and play as infancy precursors to language and theory of mind. *Cognitive Development*, *15*, 481–498.

Dunn, L. M., & Dunn, L. C. (1997). *PPVT-III: Peabody Picture Vocabulary Test—Third edition*. Circle Pines, MN: American Guidance Service.

Fenson, L., Pethick, S., Renda, C., Cox, J. L., Dale, P. S., & Reznick, J. S. (2000). Short form versions of the Macarthur Communicative Development Inventories. *Applied Psycholinguistics*, *21*, 95–115.

Garfield, J. L, Peterson, C. C., & Perry, T. (2001). Social cognition, language acquisition and the development of the theory of mind. *Mind & Language*, *16*, 494–541.

Hugues, C., & Dunn, J. (1998). Understanding mind and emotion: Longitudinal associations with mental-state talk between young friends. *Developmental Psychology*, *34*, 1026–1037.

Leslie, A. M. (1987). Pretense and representation: The origins of "theory of mind". *Psychological Review*, *94*, 412–426.

Leslie, A. M. (1994). ToMM, ToBy, and Agency: Core architecture and domain specificity. In L. Hirschfeld & S. Gelman (Eds.), *Mapping the mind: Domain specificity in cognition and culture* (pp. 119–148). New York: Cambridge University Press.

McCall, R. B., & Carriger, M. S. (1993). A meta-analysis of infant habituation and recognition memory performance as predictors of later IQ. *Child Development*, *64*, 57–79.

Meltzoff, A. N. (1995). Understanding the intentions of others: Re-enactment of intended acts by 18-month-old children. *Developmental Psychology*, *31*, 838–850.

Meltzoff, A. N., & Gopnik, A. (1993). The role of imitation in understanding persons and developing a theory of mind. In S. Baron-Cohen, H. Tager-Flusberg, & D. J. Cohen (Eds.), *Understanding other minds: Perspectives from autism* (pp. 334–366). Oxford, UK: Oxford University Press.

Olineck, K., & Poulin-Dubois, D. (2005). Infants' ability to distinguish between intentional and accidental actions and its relation to internal state language. *Infancy*, *8*, 91–100.

Perner, J., & Ruffman, T. (2005). Infants' insight into the mind: How deep? *Science*, *308*, 214–216.

Phillips, W., Baron-Cohen, S., & Rutter, M. (1998). Understanding intention in normal development and in autism. *British Journal of Developmental Psychology*, *16*, 337–348.

Phillips, A. T., Wellman, H. M., & Spelke, E. S. (2002). Infants' ability to connect gaze and emotional expression to intentional action. *Cognition*, *85*, 53–78.

Rogers, S. J., & Pennington, B. F. (1991). A theoretical approach to the deficits in infantile autism. *Development and Psychopathology*, *3*, 137–162.

Ruffman, T., Slade, L., & Crowe, E. (2002). The relation between children's and mothers' mental state language and theory-of-mind understanding. *Child Development*, *73*, 734–751.

Shatz, M., Wellman, H. M., & Silber, S. (1983). The acquisition of mental verbs: A systematic investigation of first references to mental state. *Cognition, 14*, 301–321.

Tager-Flusberg, H. (1992). Autistic children's talk about psychological states: Deficits in the early acquisition of a theory of mind. *Child Development, 63*, 161–172.

Tomasello, M. (1995). Joint attention as social cognition. In C. Moore & P. Dunham (Eds.), *Joint attention: Its origins and role in development* (pp. 85–101). Hillsdale, NJ: Lawrence Erlbaum Associates, Inc.

Tomasello, M., Carpenter, M., Call, J., Behne, T., & Moll, H. (2005). Understanding and sharing intentions: The origins of cultural cognition. *Behavioral and Brain Sciences, 28*, 675–735.

Watson, A. C., Painter, K. M., & Bornstein, M. C. (2002). Longitudinal relations between 2-year-olds' language and 4-year-olds' theory of mind. *Journal of Cognition and Development, 2*, 449–457.

Wellman, H. M., Cross, D., & Watson, J. (2001). Meta-analysis of theory-of-mind development: The truth about false-belief. *Child Development, 72*, 655–684.

Wellman, H. M., & Liu, D. (2004). Scaling of theory of mind. *Child Development, 75*, 523–541.

Wellman, H. M., Phillips, A. T., Dunphy-Lelii, S., & LaLonde, N. (2004). Infant social attention predicts preschool social cognition. *Developmental Science, 7*, 283–288.

Woodward, A. L. (1998). Infants selectively encode the goal object of an actor's reach. *Cognition, 69*, 1–34.

Woodward, A. L. (2003). Infants' developing understanding of the link between looker and object. *Developmental Science, 6*, 297–311.

Youngblade, L. M., & Dunn, J. (1995). Individual differences in young children's pretend play with mother and sibling: Links to relationships and understanding of other people's feelings and beliefs. *Child Development, 66*, 1472–1492.

EUROPEAN JOURNAL OF DEVELOPMENTAL PSYCHOLOGY
2007, 4 (1), 31–45

Differential copying of human and nonhuman models at 12 and 18 months of age

Virginia Slaughter and Danielle Corbett
University of Queensland, Brisbane, Australia

One hundred and twenty Caucasian, typically developing 12- and 18-month-old infants were presented with four models that demonstrated novel actions on objects. The model conditions were: (1) a wholly visible person; (2) disembodied human hands; (3) disembodied hands wearing mittens; and (4) disembodied mechanical pincers. Eight target actions on different objects were demonstrated in each condition. A baseline control condition was also included, in which objects were presented but no actions were demonstrated. The 12-month-olds only copied target actions above baseline when demonstrated by a person or by disembodied hands. The 18-month-olds copied all models above baseline; however, at the same time they copied the person and hands significantly more often than the other two models.

Some time around the middle of the first year of life, infants become capable of imitating others' actions on objects (Abravanel & Gingold, 1985; Barr, Dowden, & Hayne, 1996; Barr, Rovee-Collier, & Campanella, 2005; Killen & Uzgiris, 1981; Meltzoff, 1988a, 1988b; Piaget, 1962). When infants copy actions on objects that they have seen demonstrated by a model, they are potentially engaging in two concurrent activities. One is learning about the object. When a model shows how a box can be shaken to make a noise, the infant who copies the shaking action on the box has learned that the box is shakeable, and affords noise-making. At the same time, copying the box-shaking action may allow the infant to adopt the model's mindset, and communicate that mutuality (e.g., "I can shake like you"). Accordingly, most researchers acknowledge that imitation in infancy is inherently both a cognitive and a social activity (Call & Carpenter, 2002; Carpenter, 2006;

Correspondence should be addressed to Virginia Slaughter, School of Psychology, University of Queensland, Brisbane, Queensland, Australia 4072. E-mail: vps@psy.uq.edu.au
We thank Mark Nielsen for providing valuable feedback on this manuscript.

DOI: 10.1080/17405620601005622

Meltzoff & Moore, 1995; Nadel, Guérini, Pezé, & Rivet, 1999; Nielsen, 2006; Tomasello, Kruger, & Ratner, 1993; Uzgiris, 1981; Want & Harris, 2002).

Individual instances of behavioural copying vary in the extent to which they are motivated primarily by cognitive versus social functions. Further, the extent to which infants focus on the cognitive versus social aspects of a modelled action may change over development. Killen and Uzgiris (1981) showed that infants' tendencies to imitate simple actions on objects, such as banging a block on a table, changed with development, apparently in interaction with the infants' social-communicative goals. In their study, infants between the ages of 7 and 22 months were exposed to models engaging in a variety of object-directed actions. The youngest and oldest infants were most likely to copy simple acts like banging with a block, while the intermediate-aged infants did less of this type of imitation. The authors suggested that the high rates of imitation in the youngest and oldest infants reflected changing motivations to imitate: The youngest infants banged in order to master the affordances of the object, while the oldest infants, for whom banging a block was already passé, imitated instead to express mutuality with the model (e.g., "This is fun—I'll bang too").

When infants focus predominantly on affordance learning, the features of the model should matter little to their tendency to copy actions on objects, as long as those actions readily reveal what can be done with the objects. In contrast, when infants are motivated to communicate mutuality, then features of the model should interact with their willingness to copy the model's actions. Specifically, infants' tendencies to imitate should be influenced by the extent to which the model conveys social-communicative potential and displays intentions (Carpenter, Akhtar, & Tomasello, 1998; Johnson, Booth, & O'Hearn, 2001). The current study aimed to explore these hypotheses by examining patterns of copying behaviour across a range of different models, and within two different age groups.

There is considerable evidence that when infants copy actions on objects, they attend to, and are motivated by, social-communicative features of the model. For instance, Carpenter et al. (1998) reported that infants between 14 and 18 months of age were more likely to copy actions that the model verbally signalled as intentional (e.g., by saying "there" to indicate satisfactory completion) as opposed to accidental (e.g., by saying "whoops"). Similarly, 2-year-olds who observed a model opening a box were more likely to copy the model's action if they first saw her doing something that signalled her intention to get the box open (Carpenter, Call, & Tomasello, 2002).

Directly contrasting the importance of object affordance information versus the importance of a person as model, Bellagamba and Tomasello (1999) found that infants at 12 and 18 months of age were less likely to produce a target act when shown a picture portraying the end state of an already completed object-directed action, compared to seeing the action fully demonstrated by another person. The 12-month-olds did not produce the target acts at all in the absence of a human model, whereas the 18-month-olds did so, but at a significantly lower rate than when the human model demonstrated. Thus, information about object affordances alone is not always sufficient to motivate infants, in their second year of life, to copy actions on objects.

Research on imitation from television indicates that infants, between the ages of 12 and 36 months, copy actions demonstrated by a live person more often than those of a pre-recorded televised model, even when the action demonstrations are otherwise identical (Barr & Hayne, 1999; Hayne, Herbert, & Simcock, 2003). The developmental course of imitation from television is complex and may involve various perceptual and cognitive developments alongside the capacity to copy modelled actions (Barr & Hayne, 1999). However, the fact that infants are generally less likely to copy a televised model than a live person further highlights the role of social-communicative motivations in infants' copying behaviour.

At the same time, a number of recent experiments have demonstrated situations in which infants will copy actions in the absence of a social-communicative context. Huang, Heyes, and Charman (2002) showed infants pictures of objects in both their initial and end states (e.g., a chain resting outside of a bottle in one picture and the chain resting inside the bottle in a second picture), without revealing the acts that brought about the pictured transformations. When presented with the objects, 19-month-old infants produced the target acts after some exposure to the objects (e.g., the target act was typically not the first action they carried out with the object). In contrast to Bellagamba and Tomasello (1999), infants' tendencies to produce target acts in the initial and end state condition was equal to their tendency to copy a full demonstration by another person.

In another investigation of the relative importance of object affordance information versus social-communicative context to infants' tendencies to copy target acts, Huang and Charman (2005) manipulated videotapes so that 18-month-olds could see object transformations without an actor. The human body of the model was erased on the videotape so that the objects floated from initial state, through a transformation, to the end state. They found that 18-month-old infants were equally good at reproducing actions in this condition, as when they saw the actions produced by a visible actor. They argued that at 18 months, infants' exposure to the affordances of objects is sufficiently motivating for them to copy object-directed actions.

Thompson and Russell (2004) similarly found that infants between the ages of 14 and 26 months were equally likely to produce a target action whether or not the object affordance revealed by the action was demonstrated by a person. In their experiment, a novel object affordance (pushing, rather than pulling a mat to bring it close) was demonstrated by a person in the model condition, and the same affordance was demonstrated as if by magic through the surreptitious use of rods and motors in the "ghost" condition. Infants across the age range were actually more likely to produce the target action in the "ghost" condition. The authors argued that infants in the ghost condition at least, were motivated by the object affordance so they copied the novel action. This finding, together with the findings of Huang and colleagues (Huang & Charman, 2005; Huang et al., 2002), contrasts with the view that infants are most likely to copy actions demonstrated by another human.

Thus, the literature to date indicates that infants' tendencies to copy actions on objects are influenced both by social-communicative features of the model and by opportunities to learn object affordances. Infants are more likely to copy another person's actions if these are clearly goal-directed and intentional. But at the same time, infants can learn about objects by copying demonstrated actions without the presence of a social-communicative model. This complex picture reflects infants' changing motivations to imitate, as well as the presence of a number of distinct social learning mechanisms that are available to infants from the second year of life (Call & Carpenter, 2002; Nielsen, 2006).

The current study explored infants' copying behaviour, when novel actions on objects were demonstrated by models that differed in the extent to which they were recognizable as another person. Three model conditions were contrasted: hands, mittens, and pincers. These three conditions form a kind of human-ness continuum, with hands as the model most clearly human (and therefore potentially social-communicative, and goal-directed), and pincers as clearly nonhuman.

The rationale for using these different models derives from the findings of a series of studies by Woodward and colleagues, that infants before their first birthday interpret the pointing and grasping motions of hands as being goal-directed and intentional, in contrast to the motion of rigid sticks or mechanical pincers (Sommerville, Woodward, & Needham, 2005; Woodward, 1998; Woodward & Guajardo, 2002). These studies suggest that hands, in and of themselves, are interpreted as psychological agents embodying goals and intentions, either by virtue of their physical appearance and movement patterns, or by virtue of their connection to the rest of a human body. Based on this idea, we predicted that infants would readily copy novel actions on objects if these were demonstrated by human hands, since they would convey both social-communicative potential as well as object affordances.

In the current paradigm, imitation of hands can be directly contrasted with imitation of mechanical pincers, to separate information about object affordances (demonstrated equally efficiently by both pincers and hands) from the human-ness of the model. To date, there has been no test of whether infants copy actions that are demonstrated by a model that has no human or human-like features. Meltzoff (1995) reported that 18-month-old infants did not pull apart a toy dumbbell after watching a pair of mechanical pincers fail to do so; however, that study did not include a condition in which infants were shown fully consummated acts performed by the pincers. On the basis of their finding that young children copy actions demonstrated by a "ghost", Thompson and Russell (2004) predicted that when infants focus on object learning, they should be equally as likely to copy actions demonstrated by a pair of mechanical pincers as actions demonstrated by a person. The current study will test this specific prediction.

Intermediate to hands and pincers, we also included a condition in which the model is a pair of mittened hands. The mittens were morphologically comparable to the pincers in that both had only two digits with which to manipulate the objects. At the same time, they obscured the skin colour and texture of the hands inside them, which Guajardo and Woodward (2004) found was crucial to infants' interpretation of hands as intentional and goal-directed. Based on Guajardo and Woodward's (2004) finding, we predicted that the younger infants, at least, would not readily copy actions demonstrated by mittens. Thus, we will refer to both the pincers and the mittens as "nonhuman" models.

Finally, we also included a whole person condition, which acted as a kind of upper baseline, given that imitation is most natural in response to another, wholly visible, person's activity. The lower baseline was a standard condition in which the objects were introduced but not manipulated by a fully visible person before presentation to the infant. This allowed us to measure and control for spontaneous production of target actions.

METHOD

Participants

Participants were 120 full-term infants including 60 12-month-olds (32 boys, 28 girls; mean age = 364 days, $SD = 11$ days) and 60 18-month-olds (30 boys, 30 girls; mean age = 540 days, $SD = 10$ days). Infants were recruited by letter from birth announcements and a laboratory database of willing participants. All infants were typically developing, according to their parents, and within 14 days of their 12- or 18-month birthday when tested.

Design

Twelve infants in each age group were randomly assigned to one of the five conditions.

In the *baseline* condition, a fully visible person sat quietly while target objects were introduced, but without touching them. In the experimental conditions, infants watched a model perform target actions on objects. The models included: (1) a fully visible female *person*; (2) two human *hands* that protruded thorough a screen; (3) two hands dressed in cream-coloured woollen *mittens* with a red leaf motif; and (4) a pair of grey, blue and pink mechanical *pincers*.

There were equal numbers of male and female infants in each group, except the 12-month-old "person" group for which there were 8 males and 4 females. Infants in each group, were given 8 target objects, presentation of which was randomized within and across groups.

Materials

Infants sat in a high chair and a parent sat beside them, facing a rectangular table (151 × 91 cm). Across the table opposite the infant and parent was the model. A video camera behind and to the left of the model recorded the infant's head, torso, and a portion of the tabletop where the test objects were manipulated.

Opposite to the seated infant and parent hung a black screen that spanned the width of the table and extended from the ceiling to the floor. The screen had inconspicuous openings so that a model sitting behind it could put her hands (which could be naked, or else wearing mittens) or the pair of robotic pincers through the screen so that the infant could only see the protrusions (Figure 1). Also embedded in the screen was a 30 cm strip of black gauze that ran horizontally across the screen at the model's eye height, so that she could see her hands or the pincers while manipulating the test objects. The infant could not see through any part of the screen, so he or she could be presented with effectively disembodied hands, mittens or pincers, that manipulated objects on the table. In the "person" condition, the model sat in front of the screen.

There were 8 target objects with which models demonstrated novel actions. The first 5 were similar to those used in Meltzoff (1995). An additional three objects were constructed. The majority of objects were either hand made or store-bought items that were modified, so that the infant could not have played with them before. The rest of the objects were purchased items that were used in novel ways, so that the infants were unlikely to be familiar with the target actions.

Dumbbell. The first object resembled a dumbbell, consisting of a red wooden cube at either end of an 8.5 cm yellow PVC covered piece of dowel. The dowel fitted snugly inside holes bored in the wooden cubes so that the cubes do not accidentally fall off due to banging or shaking of the dumbbell.

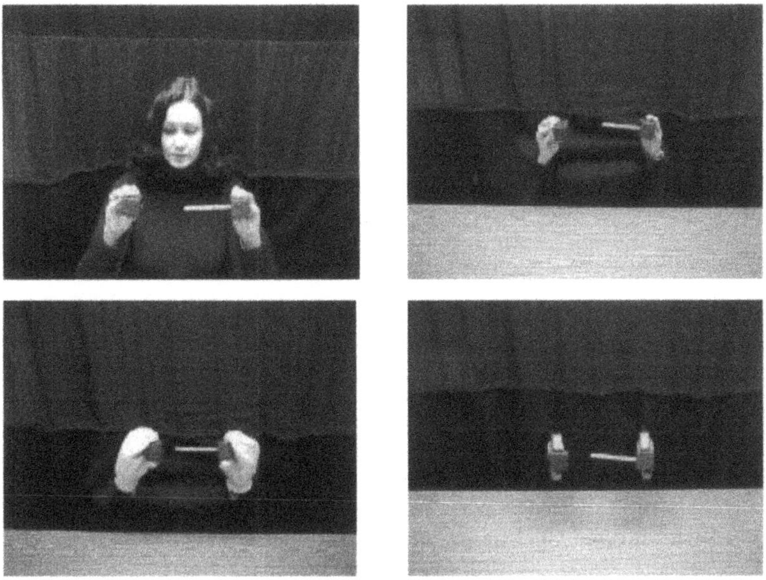

Figure 1. Human and nonhuman models presented to infants: person (top left), hands (top right), mittens (bottom left) and pincers (bottom right).

Cubes were used in this experiment as opposed to balls, as the cubes facilitated ease of manipulation by the pincers. The target action for the dumbbell was holding the wooden cubes at either end and pulling outwards until it was in two pieces.

Bottle and chain. The second object was a (177 ml) baby's bottle with the teat removed, and a gold coloured chain (20.5 cm in length when suspended) with a gold pendant. The target action was to hold the chain over the opening and then lower it all the way into the bottle until the chain rested on the bottom.

Prong and loop. This was a horizontally-mounted wooden green prong protruding from an upright piece of wood, and a white plastic chain loop (20 cm in length when suspended). The prong had a 2.5 cm diameter and protruded 5.5 cm from the piece of wood on which it was mounted. The target action was to drape the chain over the prong.

Cube and post. This was an 8×1.5 cm diameter piece of dowel positioned upright in the centre of a square wooden base (9.5 cm square and 2 cm deep), and a cube ($6.25 \times 5.5 \times 5.5$ cm) with a 2 cm diameter hole bored through the middle. The target action was to lower the cube over the dowel until the cube rested on the base and the dowel protruded through hole in the cube.

Buzzer box and stick. The fifth object was a small box (18 × 18 × 3 cm) with a slightly recessed rectangular button (3 × 3 cm), which when pressed activated a buzzer inside the box. The stick was a 2 × 2 cm square piece of dowel, 10 cm in length. The target action was to push the button with the stick to make the buzzer sound.

Rattle and rake. A plastic rake (26 cm in length) and a rattle (18 × 11 cm) comprised this object set. The target action was to use the rake as a tool to access a rattle placed out of arm's reach.

Shake box. This was a pink box, the inside of which was lined with cotton wool. It also contained a metal sinker connected to a rubber band, the two ends of which were fixed to the inside of the box. Hence, the sinker hung in the middle of the box and would not make a sound unless the target action was performed. The target action was to shake the box on its side with sufficient force to produce a noise.

Hammer and blocks. These were a blue Lego block (7 × 3 × 2 cm) with a red Lego block (13 × 2 × 3 cm) connected to the top of it, and a wooden hammer (18 cm long × 6 cm width of hammer head). The target action was to hit the red block repeatedly with the hammer.

Procedure

Infants were placed in a high chair with a parent seated next to them. An assistant sat at one end of the table between the infant and model, and was responsible for presenting objects to the model for demonstration and then to the infant for the response period. Infants were accompanied by a parent for the duration of the study.

For each condition, the assistant brought the objects one by one from a hidden box. Each was placed on the table in front of the model, who performed the target action three times, except in the baseline condition, when the model sat quietly and the objects remained in front of her on the table for approximately the same amount of time that the action demonstration would have taken. For each trial, after the target action was demonstrated, the assistant took the object from the model, rested it under the table for 1 second, then placed it on the table in front of the infant. The infant then had a 20 second response period, timed starting from when the infant first touched the object.

Scoring

Target action production. Infants were given a score of 1 if the target action (exactly as described above for each object) was performed at least once during the 20 second test period. Some of the 12-month-olds first explored the objects with their mouths before engaging in manual exploration of the objects, so were given an extra 10 seconds (as in Bellagamba & Tomasello, 1999).

Visual attention. Infants' visual attention to the different models was measured as a control to ensure that infants had equivalent exposure to the actions performed across conditions. Since modelling demonstrations varied slightly from trial to trial, we calculated the proportion of time each infant watched every object demonstration, beginning when the model first touched the object, and ending when the model released the object after the third target act was demonstrated.

Reliability

All scoring was done by the second author. Reliability of target action scores was assessed by having an independent observer (blind to condition) rescore 25% of the infants in each age group. There was 98% agreement between the two scorers.

RESULTS

Production of target actions was summed across the eight objects so that each infant received a single score ranging from 0 to 8. Figure 2 illustrates the rates of target action production in response to each model, by age group.

Which models do infants copy?

Our first analysis revealed which of the models inspired copying by infants at each age. To accomplish this, we performed planned *t*-tests comparing scores in each model condition to target action scores in the baseline condition where nothing was demonstrated. This was done separately for the two age groups.

Twelve-month-olds significantly imitated both person (mean score = 3.58, $SD = 1.73$) and hands (mean score = 4.33, $SD = 2.10$) above the baseline level (mean score = 1.42, $SD = 1.08$), both $ts > 3.68$, $ps < .01$. Imitation of mittens by 12-month-olds (mean score = 2.42, $SD = 1.44$) was not significantly above baseline, $t(22) = 1.92$, $p = .069$. Imitation of the pincers

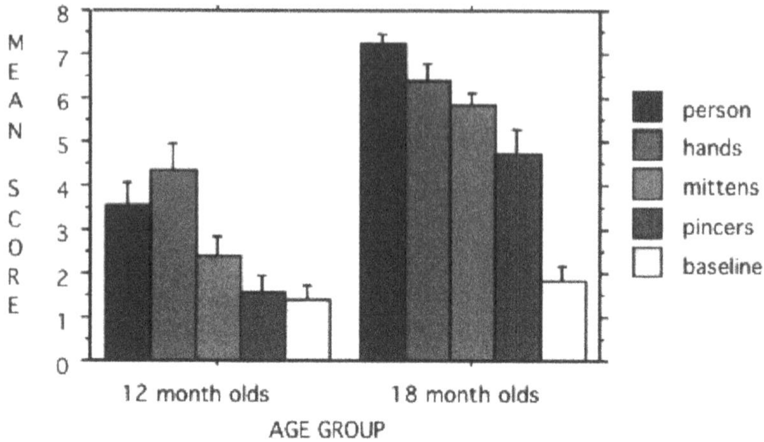

Figure 2. Mean imitation scores (out of 8) by condition and age. Error bars represent standard errors.

(mean score = 1.58, $SD = 1.31$) was also not significantly above baseline in the sample of 12-month-olds, $t(22) = 0.74$, *ns*. This pattern indicates that only the hands and person engendered imitative responses in the 1-year-old infants.

Among the 18-month-olds, imitation scores were significantly above baseline in all four model conditions, all $ts(22) > 4.84$, $ps < .001$. The mean scores and standard deviations for the 18-month-olds were as follows: baseline = 1.83 ($SD = 1.11$); person = 7.25 ($SD = 0.75$); hands = 6.40 ($SD = 1.24$); mittens = 5.83 ($SD = 0.94$); pincers = 4.75 ($SD = 1.76$). These data indicate that the 18-month-olds imitated the actions demonstrated by all of the models.

Do infants imitate all models equally?

The next analysis compared imitation rates across the four models by age group. We computed a 2 (Age Group: 12 and 18 months) × 4 (Model: person, hands, mittens, pincers) ANOVA in which imitation score (out of a maximum of 8) was the dependent variable. This analysis revealed a significant main effect of age, $F(1, 88) = 105.40$, $p < .001$, that reflected 18-month-olds' greater tendency to imitate across all the models. There was also a significant main effect of model, $F(3, 88) = 13.02$, $p < .01$. Follow-up Tukey–Kramer post hoc tests comparing imitation rates across the four models revealed that imitation of the person and hands was equal, and those were both significantly greater than imitation of mittens and pincers. Rates of imitation of mittens and pincers were not different. There was no interaction of age and model.

Attention to the models

Before directly interpreting these differential results across models, it was important to ensure that infants attended to all of the models. A 2 (Age) × 4 (Condition: person, hands, mittens, pincers) ANOVA on the proportion of time infants spent looking directly at the demonstrating model produced no significant main effects or interactions, indicating that infants attended equally to each of the models. Proportions of visual attention to the models ranged from 0.97 to 1.00 across conditions and age groups. Thus, any differences in infants' tendencies to copy the models cannot be attributed to their simply being more or less interested in watching them produce actions on objects.

DISCUSSION

This study demonstrated developmental changes in infants' tendencies to copy human and nonhuman models. The 12-month-olds copied actions demonstrated by a person and a person's disembodied hands at equal rates. However, at 12 months of age infants did not copy actions modelled by mittened hands, or mechanical pincers. The 18-month-olds, in contrast, copied all four models. At the same time, the 18-month-olds' rates of copying of person and hands were significantly greater than their rates of copying of mittens and pincers.

The findings first of all contradict Thompson and Russell's (2004) suggestion that infants would happily copy actions demonstrated by mechanical pincers. At both ages, infants' were significantly less likely to copy mittens or pincers than hands, even though the target action demonstrations were otherwise identical. The fact that the 12-month-olds in the current study exhibited no tendency to copy the nonhuman models is somewhat reminiscent of Killen and Uzgiris' (1981) finding that their intermediate-aged infants did not copy target actions that both younger and older infants did produce. Like Killen and Uzgiris' 10-month-olds, the 12-month-olds in the current study were physically capable of producing the actions that were demonstrated by the mittens and pincers, however they did not do so.

There are two possible explanations for this pattern of responding that are not mutually exclusive. The first is that at 12 months, infants are not sufficiently motivated by object affordances alone, to copy actions produced by nonhuman models. That is, the 1-year-olds copied the person and hands because they were recognizably human and therefore clearly goal-directed and potentially social. But these younger infants were not motivated to copy target actions when the model had no human features. On this view, even if the object affordances were obvious in the mitten and pincer condition, infants would have failed to copy the demonstrated actions because they were not produced by a potentially social, communicative other. This explanation is consistent with Bellagamba and Tomasello's (1999) finding that 12-month-olds produced target actions on objects only when another person demonstrated the action, whereas 18-month-olds were also able to produce target acts (albeit at a lower rate) from simply seeing the final outcome of the action (e.g., the objects' affordance).

However, there are also recent demonstrations of pure outcome-copying in 1-year-old infants, that challenge this explanation. The youngest infants to reproduce the action demonstrated by magic in Thompson and Russell's (2004) "ghost" condition were 14 months of age. These infants copied an action that was demonstrated without any model. Also relevant is Nielsen's (2006) finding that when 12-month-olds were presented with a complex box-opening task that required using a tool, the majority of them abandoned the tool and simply opened the box with their hands. In this instance, 12-months-olds were clearly more motivated by the boxes' affordances, than by a desire to be like the model.

The other possible explanation for the 12-month-olds' failure to copy the mittens and pincers is that they were simply unable to learn object affordances from those nonhuman models. This might be because the mittens and pincers were physically dissimilar to the infants' own bodies, since both of those models had only two digits with which to manipulate objects. As a result, the 12-month-olds may have found it difficult to interpret the demonstrated actions and translate them into their own matching behaviours. Given that infants of 12 months have limited knowledge about the structure of the human body in general (Slaughter & Heron, 2004), this may be a viable explanation for their differential copying.

The pattern of results for the 18-month-olds in the current study is subject to two explanations, along the lines of those for the 12-month-olds, and again not mutually exclusive. Eighteen-month-olds were able to learn object affordances from all the models, evidenced by their above-baseline copying across all model conditions. This finding is consistent with Huang and Charman (2005) and Thompson and Russell (2004), who also found that infants could readily learn object affordances and therefore reproduce target acts, without a human model to demonstrate them. However, the differential copying of human versus nonhuman models that we observed in the 18-month-olds is inconsistent with Huang and Charman (2005) and Thompson and Russell (2004). In both of those studies, infants' production of target acts was equivalent whether demonstrated with or without the human model. In the current study, by contrast, when the model was nonhuman, then the rate of copying was significantly decreased relative to the human models. One explanation for this pattern is that the nonhuman appearance of the mittens and pincers actually disrupted 18-month-olds' ability or motivation to learn the object affordances being demonstrated, so that their copying was depressed in response to these models. On this view, both the 12- and 18-month-olds were less likely to copy actions demonstrated by mittens and pincers because they had trouble learning object affordances from these models, compared to the human models.

An alternative explanation for the 18-month-olds' differential responding across model conditions is that when the model was a human or human hands, infants were motivated not only by what they saw the objects could do, but by the social-communicative potential of the human models. That is, the 18-month-olds learned the object affordances from all the models, but may have been further motivated to copy the human and hands models because these offered, on top of learning about the objects, some additional potential for recognition and communication of mutuality. This interpretation is generally consistent with Killen and Uzgiris' (1981) proposal that older infants copied simple actions on objects mainly in order to be social, rather than to learn object affordances. It is also consistent with the developmental course of synchronic imitation, which emerges between 15 and 18 months of age, and is recognized as a form of copying behaviour that is driven purely by social-communicative motivations (Nielsen & Dissanayake, 2004). Thus, the older infants' differential copying may have come about because at 18 months, affordance learning interacts with infants' desire to communicate with potentially social models.

The results of this study support Woodward's claim, based on younger infants' visual responses to hands, that within the first year of life hands themselves are recognized as embodying goals and intentions. At both 12 and 18 months, infants were equally as likely to copy actions demonstrated by disembodied hands, as they were to copy the actions of a fully visible person. Whether this construal is based on an understanding that human hands are driven by a human mind, or else based on some sort of learned association between the form of manual gestures and their outcomes (as suggested by Woodward, 1998) is a question that requires further investigation.

Overall the pattern of data in the current study supports the idea that imitation in infancy reflects an interaction of social and cognitive motivations. For the 12-month-olds, learning about object affordances was only evident if the model was another human. The 18-month-olds learned object affordances from all of the models but at the same time, they were more likely to copy actions if the model had human features. The significance of the person and hands as imitative models may have operated in both the cognitive and social domains: The human models may have engendered recognition of similarity between model and infant, which facilitated their learning how to manipulate the target objects. At the same time, the human models embodied some potential for social interaction and communication that may have further motivated infants to copy what they did.

REFERENCES

Abravanel, E., & Gingold, H. (1985). Learning via observation during the second year of life. *Developmental Psychology, 21*, 614–623.

Barr, R., Dowden, A., & Hayne, H. (1996). Developmental changes in deferred imitation by 6- to 24-month-old infants. *Infant Behaviour and Development, 19*, 159–171.

Barr, R., & Hayne, H. (1999). Developmental changes in imitation from television during infancy. *Child Development, 70*, 1067–1081.

Barr, R., Rovee-Collier, C., & Campanella, J. (2005). Retrieval protracts deferred imitation by 6-month-olds. *Infancy, 7*, 263–283.

Bellagamba, F., & Tomasello, M. (1999). Re-enacting intended acts: Comparing 12- and 18-month-olds. *Infant Behaviour and Development, 22*, 277–282.

Call, J., & Carpenter, M. (2002). Three sources of information in social learning. In K. Dautenhahn & C. Nehaniv (Eds.), *Imitation in animals and artefacts* (pp. 211–228). Cambridge, MA: MIT Press.

Carpenter, M. (2006). Instrumental, social, and shared goals and intentions in imitation. In S. J. Rogers & J. H. G. Williams (Eds.), *Imitation and the development of the social mind: Lessons from typical development and autism* (pp. 48–70). New York: Guilford Press.

Carpenter, M., Akhtar, N., & Tomasello, M. (1998). 14- through 18-month-old infants differentially imitate intentional and accidental actions. *Infant Behavior and Development, 21*, 315–330.

Carpenter, M., Call, J., & Tomasello, M. (2002). Understanding "prior intentions" enables 2-year-olds to imitatively learn a complex task. *Child Development, 73*, 1431–1441.

Guajardo, J., & Woodward, A. (2004). Is agency skin-deep? Surface attributes influence infants' sensitivity to goal-directed action. *Infancy, 6*, 361–384.

Hayne, H., Herbert, J., & Simcock, G. (2003). Imitation from television by 24- and 30-month-olds. *Developmental Science, 6*, 254–261.

Huang, C.-T., & Charman, T. (2005). Gradations of emulation learning in infants' imitation of actions on objects. *Journal of Experimental Child Psychology, 92*, 276–302.

Huang, C.-T., Heyes, C., & Charman, T. (2002). Infants' behavioral re-enactment of "failed attempts": Exploring the roles of emulation learning, stimulus enhancement and understanding of intentions. *Developmental Psychology, 38*, 840–855.

Johnson, S., Booth, A., & O'Hearn, K. (2001). Inferring the unseen goals of a nonhuman agent. *Cognitive Development, 16*, 637–656.

Killen, M., & Uzgiris, I. (1981). Imitation of actions with objects: The role of social meaning. *Journal of Genetic Psychology, 138*, 219–229.

Meltzoff, A. (1988a). Infant imitation after a 1-week delay: Long-term memory for novel acts and multiple stimuli. *Developmental Psychology, 24*, 470–476.

Meltzoff, A. (1988b). Infant imitation and memory: Nine-month-olds in immediate and deferred tests. *Child Development, 59*, 217–225.

Meltzoff, A. (1995). Understanding the intentions of others: Re-enactment of intended acts by 18-month-old children. *Developmental Psychology, 31*, 838–850.

Meltzoff, A., & Moore, M. (1995). Infants' understanding of people and things: From body imitation to folk psychology. In J. Bermúdez, A. J. Marcel, & N. Eilan (Eds.), *The body and the self* (pp. 43–69). Cambridge, MA: MIT Press.

Nadel, J., Guérini, C., Pezé, A., & Rivet, C. (1999). The evolving nature of imitation as a format for communication. In J. Nadel & G. Butterworth (Eds.), *Imitation in infancy* (pp. 209–234). Cambridge, UK: Cambridge University Press.

Nielsen, M. (2006). Copying actions and copying outcomes: Social learning through the second year. *Developmental Psychology, 42*, 555–565.

Nielsen, M., & Dissanayake, C. (2004). Pretend play, mirror self-recognition and imitation: A longitudinal investigation through the second year. *Infant Behavior and Development, 27*, 342–365.

Piaget, J. (1962). *Play, dreams and imitation in childhood.* New York: W. W. Norton.

Slaughter, V., & Heron, M. (2004). Origins and early development of human body knowledge. *Monographs of the Society for Research in Child Development.* Serial number 276, *69*(2).

Sommerville, J., Woodward, A., & Needham, A. (2005). Action experience alters 3-month-old infants' perception of others' actions. *Cognition, 96*, B1–B11.

Thompson, D., & Russell, J. (2004). The ghost condition: Imitation versus emulation in young children's observational learning. *Developmental Psychology, 40*, 882–889.

Tomasello, M., Kruger, A., & Ratner, H. (1993). Cultural learning. *Behavioral and Brain Sciences, 16*, 495–552.

Uzgiris, I. (1981). Two functions of imitation during infancy. *International Journal of Behavioral Development, 4*, 1–12.

Want, S. C., & Harris, P. L. (2002). How do children ape? Applying concepts from the study of nonhuman primates to the developmental study of "imitation" in human children. *Developmental Science, 5*, 1–13.

Woodward, A. (1998). Infants selectively encode the goal object of an actor's reach. *Cognition, 69*, 1–34.

Woodward, A., & Guajardo, J. (2002). Infants' understanding of the point gesture as an object-directed action. *Cognitive Development, 17*, 1061–1084.

EUROPEAN JOURNAL OF DEVELOPMENTAL PSYCHOLOGY
2007, 4 (1), 46–64

Social cognition in infancy: A critical review of research on higher order abilities

Sylvain Sirois and Iain Jackson
The University of Manchester, UK

This paper reviews early precursors to social cognition in infancy, then critically reviews infancy work suggesting goal attribution to human agents in the first year of life and theory of mind (ToM) abilities (assessed through a modified false belief task) in the second year of life. Overall, methodological problems and statistical limitations compound data interpretation, which would be equivocal despite these limitations. The authors find no support for high-order social cognitive abilities in infancy. The discussion focuses on how the field of social cognition in infancy should build theories from the bottom up, assessing how simpler precursors change over time and combine to give rise to socially competent individuals.

INTRODUCTION

A defining trait of humans is our intensely social nature. We, as adults, understand others as intentional beings with beliefs and desires (Wellman, Phillips, Dunphy-Lelii, & LaLonde, 2004). Not surprisingly, given the importance of social interactions, the emerging field of social brain sciences has identified a variety of cortical areas specialized for processing social information (Adolphs, 2003). However, nonhuman primates (especially apes) also show a range of social cognitive abilities. For example, young chimpanzees exhibit face recognition, smiling, gazing, but not triadic (self–other–object) interactions (Tomonaga et al., 2004). Nevertheless, a proper theory of mind (ToM) appears to be a unique human ability.

Correspondence should be addressed to Sylvain Sirois, School of Psychological Sciences, The University of Manchester, Oxford Road, Manchester M13 9PL, UK.
E-mail: sylvain.sirois@manchester.ac.uk

This work was supported in part by a 1 + 3 postgraduate studentship from The Economic and Social Research Council (ESRC) to the second author.

DOI: 10.1080/17405620601047053

The last two decades have seen a growing number of infancy studies about the emergence of social cognitive behaviours. Like other areas of infancy research (e.g., Haith, 1998; Spelke, 1999), this work has developed an ongoing nature–nurture debate. Some researchers argue that there are specific, innately specified cognitive mechanisms for the processing of social information, such as the ToM module (Leslie, 2005). Others argue that simple precursors of adult abilities exist, but only serve to steer social interactions in order to help develop the actual abilities (Nadel, Prepin, & Okanda, 2004; Wellman et al., 2004). A radical version of the developmental approach to social cognition proposes that precursors only serve to fool adults into investing in the infant (i.e., infants as social impersonators), which indirectly bootstraps infants into social interactions from which they will acquire the actual social cognitive skills that may causally have nothing to do with the precursors (Povinelli, Prince, & Preuss, 2005).

In this paper, we begin with a brief review of some of the core precursors of social behaviour, such as face perception, joint attention, and imitation. We then critically review recent infant data suggesting precocious abilities for complex social thinking. We first examine data about goal attribution in infants (e.g., Gergely, Nadasdy, Csibra, & Biro, 1995; Woodward, 1998), and then review some initial data on ToM (Onishi & Baillargeon, 2005). In both areas, we find that the results (which stem from looking-time data in violation-of-expectation paradigms) are equivocal due to methodological confounds, statistical limitations, or alternative interpretations. We argue that claims of complex social cognition in infants are, at best, premature. The discussion focuses on the tension between bottom-up and top-down research paradigms for research on social cognition in infancy.

EARLY PRECURSORS OF THE SOCIAL MIND

The ability to act socially with conspecifics obviously requires, a priori, the identification of such individuals. In human infants, it is relatively well established that newborns will preferentially attend to face-like stimuli (relative to similar stimuli that do not show the specific spatial organization of eyes and mouth) within the first few minutes of birth (Goren, Sarty, & Wu, 1975; Johnson, Dziurawiec, Ellis, & Morton, 1991). Newborns' eye and head movements were similar when tracking a drawing of a face and a configuration of three blobs positioned as eyes and mouth, relative to spatial combinations of these features that reorganized the position of features or blobs. An interpretation of these data, dubbed CONSPEC, proposes that newborns are endowed with minimal structural information about faces so that in a normal environment they would orient towards faces (Morton & Johnson, 1991). Importantly, this endowment does not include a detailed specification of human faces. Morton and Johnson (1991) argue that such richer representations are derived empirically from a CONLEARN device, a learning process used to derive characteristics of conspecifics. CONLEARN functionally takes over from CONSPEC at about two months post partum. The idea is that CONSPEC biases the infant's environment (through more attention to faces), helping the brain to acquire a specialization for own-species face processing. Developmental comparative data with chimpanzees support this suggestion (Myowa-Yamakoshi, Yamaguchi, Tomonaga, Tanaka, & Matsuzawa, 2005).

In a landmark study by Meltzoff and Moore (1977), newborns were assessed on their ability to imitate various facial expressions from an adult. They found that newborns imitated above chance several facial gestures, the most salient of which was tongue protrusion (TP). Although this work has been replicated by varied researchers across a range of behaviours (including vocalization), some researchers have failed to find supportive data for newborn imitation (Anisfeld et al., 2001). The interpretation of neonate imitation, especially TP, remains controversial nearly 30 years on. It is worth noting that tongue protrusion, the hallmark measure of imitation, is perhaps best understood as an exploratory function (Jones, 1996), which in ambiguous social contexts is relied upon up to 4 months of age, when TP become superseded by reaching (Chen, Reid, & Striano, 2006).

Social smiling (i.e., whereby the infant smiles contingently to the behaviour of someone else) typically emerges between 6 and 8 weeks after birth. Prior to social smiling, infant smiles appear to be mainly reflexive and are observed in limited circumstances such as REM sleep (Emde & Koenig, 1969). But when social smiling emerges, infants quickly adapt it as a function of a range of stimulus features (Hains & Muir, 1996; Watson, 1972). What is important to note is that such smiling does not entail advanced social understanding on the part of the infant, an issue that is orthogonal to potential increased bonding in rewarded caregivers (Povinelli et al., 2005).

In the second half of the first year of life, the ability of infants to follow the gaze of others develops substantially (Butterworth & Jarrett, 1991; Scaife & Bruner, 1975). Although initially limited to simple linear searches within their visual field, by 12 months infants can encode the relation between the adult's gaze and their own and carry out geometric searches within their visual field. Between 12 and 18 months, infants acquire the ability to use adult gazes to areas beyond their own visual field (Butterworth & Jarrett, 1991).

The emergence of gaze following allows infants to engage in a range of behaviours that fall under the umbrella of the term joint attention (Carpendale, Lewis, Muller, & Racine, 2004). However, gaze following is but one aspect of joint attention, and the exact *what* and *when* of joint attention remain controversial (Carpendale et al., 2004). Controversy aside, the importance of joint attention cannot be overstated (Tomasello, Carpenter, Call, Behne, & Moll, 2005). For instance, it has been argued that joint attention is a necessary precursor to language acquisition (Tomasello, 2003). We return to joint attention in the section on ToM.

During the first two years of life, a host of socially relevant abilities have thus been identified in infants. They have means to identify and learn about conspecifics, with whom they can interact by means of imitation and social smiling. They progressively acquire the ability to use the gaze of others to parse the environment, ultimately engaging in joint attention activities. All of these suggest that humans build the required information-processing machinery for social interaction during infancy, but do not imply that early social behaviour is socially intentional. The next two sections review infancy work that explicitly aims to examine the intentional nature of infants' minds.

INFANTS' UNDERSTANDING OF GOAL

Attributing goals to others is an essential aspect of adults' social lives. We can use purported goals to predict the behaviour of others, or to alter our own behaviour adaptively. Furthermore, we can attempt to change others' goals or inaccurately display our own goals to our own advantage. Research on goal attribution in infants was influenced by initial work from Woodward (1998, 1999). We examine these two initial papers, and then review ongoing work within this paradigm.

In her seminal paper, Woodward (1998) first habituates infants to a scene where either a human actor reaches into a stage to grasp one of two toys, or where an inanimate claw does the same. In the test trials the position of the toys was switched and the infants in each condition then saw the same agent reach for either the same toy, and therefore move through a different path, or the other toy, along the original path. The results showed that 5-, 6-, and 9-month-old infants looked significantly longer when the path of the human arm remained the same but a new toy, or "goal", was grasped than when an old goal was grasped following a new path of movement. This was inferred by Woodward to represent the infant's awareness of the functional relationship between the actor's hand and goal. Furthermore, as no looking differences were found between the test trials of the rod or claw conditions, infants are suggested to be aware to attribute goal-directed behaviours only to human actions. Table 1 summarizes the pattern of data from this study, dichotomizing between short and long looking times to test items.

However, we suggest that the above explanation does not adequately reveal the complete picture of the observed data. Woodward's (1998) test items follow a factorial design crossing agent (arm vs rod) and target (new toy vs old toy). A proper analysis would have initially examined for a significant interaction (of which there likely was one). More importantly,

TABLE 1
Pattern of looking times on test items from Woodward (1998). The pattern is identical in Woodward (1999), where "human arm" is replaced by "grasping hand" and "rod/claw" is replaced by "palm-up hand"

	Target	
Agent	*Old toy*	*New toy*
Human arm	Short	Long
Rod/claw	Long	Long

pairwise comparisons between looking times within rows of Table 1, as were carried out because this was the experimental hypothesis, would have been complemented with pairwise comparisons within columns, which completely changes the picture. The selective use of cross-condition comparisons has been discussed elsewhere (e.g., Bogartz, Shinskey & Speaker, 1997), but it is notable that what we observe in that paper appears to be a confirmation bias from top-down research goals at the expense of a thorough examination of the empirical data. Indeed, we suggest that the data might be better explained by turning the given explanation on its head; rather than infants showing *increased* looking towards the human arm grasping a new toy, the overall data would appear to indicate a *reduction* in looking in test trials where the human arm reaches for the old toy in its new position, relative to the other three test trial conditions.

According to this alternative interpretation, a low-level perceptual explanation obscures the conclusion that infants selectively apply a "store of knowledge" to "goal related" events. One can easily argue that the relative salience of toys after habituation is unaffected by the arm (a familiar stimulus) but is affected by a rod or claw (an unfamiliar stimulus), or vice-versa. Indeed, the use of terminology such as "goal", rather than simply toy, somewhat presupposes the nature of infants' representations and inadvertently distracts from alternative interpretations.

Woodward (1999) also investigated whether 5- and 9-month-old infants distinguish between goal-directed and non-purposeful behaviour. In a similar experimental design to her 1998 experiments, infants were habituated to one of two conditions. In the first condition, an actor reached into a stage and lowered her hand to rest grasping one of two toys. In the other condition, the actor reached into the stage and lowered her hand in an unintentional manner to rest palm up on one of the toys. The rationale here is that palm up contact with a toy would not be construed as goal directed by infants, contrasting with the grasping condition. As before, test trials crossed two factors: target (new vs old) and purposefulness (grasp vs palm up). The pattern of results for infants of 9 months of age was identical to the one reported in Table 1, and was construed by Woodward (1999) as indicating that infants interpreted the actions in terms of goal attribution. A similar pattern of results was obtained for 5-month-olds, but did not reach significance.

Direct comparisons of the results across the two series of experiments is hindered by the use of different measures of central tendency (median vs mean) and spread (median absolute deviations vs standard error of mean) between papers. However, we suggest that the same limitations in the analysis of results apply to both papers, and that both interpretations of goal attribution confound similar perceptual interpretations. Indeed, the grasping hand (familiar in interaction with objects) or the palm-up hand (unfamiliar in that context) could have affected the relative salience of old and new toys. We thus fail to see convincing, unequivocal evidence of goal attribution in infants in these two studies.

In an extension of this paradigm, Sommerville and Woodward habituated 12-month-old infants to a scene where an actor pulled a cloth towards her and then retrieved a toy (Sommerville & Woodward, 2005). For about half of the infants, the toy had been on the cloth and was pulled with it (see Figure 1). For the remaining infants, the toy had been next to the cloth and was moved by the actor's hand after the cloth was moved (see Figure 2). Test trials saw the actor pick a new toy after using the same cloth, or pick the old toy using a new cloth (bottom rows of Figures 1 and 2). Analyses this time were applied to a nested design with two factors: target toy (new vs old, a within-subject factor) and condition (toy-on-cloth vs toy-off-cloth, a between-subject factor). Data showed that infants looked longer at an event in which a new toy on the same cloth as in habituation trials was pulled closer by an actor ("new goal event") than when the same toy as in habituation trials was pulled closer when it rested on a different cloth ("new means event"). There was no looking time difference observed in "control" events when the toys sat adjacent to the cloths rather than on them. Although the design is logically equivalent to Woodward's (1998, 1999) previous work as far as analyses are concerned, it is worth pointing out that the pattern of results differs from what is reported in Table 1. Indeed, both *long* values in the last row should be changed to *short*.

From these results Sommerville and Woodward (2005) conclude that infants "understand that the initial step of cloth-pulling sequence is directed toward the ultimate goal of attaining the toy" (p. 1) and form "goal attributions" from inferences about the actor's behaviour. Sommerville and Woodward (2005) suggest that their control condition is sufficient to allow the conclusion that the looking preference was not due to the "construction of [a] simple perceptual rule" (p. 13). However, the "control" event merely showed an actor moving the toy towards them, rather than the toy being pulled closer on the cloth. If the only variable infants are sensitive to is

Figure 1. Habituation (top row) and test events (bottom row) for the toy-on-cloth condition. (From Sommerville, J. A., & Woodward, A. L., 2005, Pulling out the intentional structure of action: The relation between action processing and action production in infancy, *Cognition*, *95*, 1–30. Copyright 2005, reprinted with permission from Elsevier.)

simple motion of the toy this might indeed suffice. Perceptually, however, the two events cannot be considered equivalent. Furthermore, the failure to investigate looking-time differences across all combinations of test (i.e., new toy paired with new cloth, and same cloth paired with same toy, are absent from the design) and conditions does not allow for the elimination of the effect of confounding variables, and certainly does not suggest that we ought to make assumptions for infants' ability to represent abstract mental states. Whereas a proper analysis of variance was carried out in this paper, the significant interaction was subsequently examined for only those looking-time pairs consistent with the research hypothesis. Again, crucial analyses that would likely alter the interpretation of data are missing. And the

Figure 2. Habituation (top row) and test events (bottom row) for the toy-off-cloth condition. (From Sommerville, J. A., & Woodward, A. L., 2005, Pulling out the intentional structure of action: The relation between action processing and action production in infancy, *Cognition*, *95*, 1–30. Copyright 2005, reprinted with permission from Elsevier.)

discrepancy with earlier work (Woodward, 1998, 1999) as far as the general pattern of results is concerned is not examined.

Without such statistical controls it is difficult to see the justification for inferences that "infants are not merely associating actions within a sequence based upon their temporal continuity, but rather use top-down knowledge to influence the extent to which they rely on statistical regularity in their action processing" (Sommerville & Woodward, 2005, p. 13). On the contrary, the data they refer to can be construed to show infants' ability to form statistical associations, with the idea of goal attribution remaining an open question. In fact, as Gergely (2001) observes, researchers who intend to demonstrate that infants' representations rely on top-down, higher level processing should be required to design experimental demonstrations that explicitly go beyond the reach of simple, perceptual, associationist accounts.

Another approach to studying the understanding of goals in infants is the rational–irrational path paradigm proposed by Gergely and colleagues (1995). In this research, 12-month-old infants were shown short, 2D film sequences showing an agent approaching a goal. In the rational condition, the agent made a detour around an obstacle. In the irrational condition, a similar detour was made in the absence of an obstacle. Infants in each condition were habituated to the relevant event, then tested on direct and indirect approaches in the absence of an obstacle. Infants looked longer to test events when the rational agent made an unnecessary detour (albeit using a familiar path), whereby infants paid comparable attention to either path in the irrational condition. Similar results have been obtained with 9- but not 6-month-olds (Csibra, Gergely, Biro, Koos, & Brockbank, 1999), and in 1-year-olds using complex visual events (Sodian, Schoeppner, & Metz, 2004).

Gergely and colleagues explained these data by suggesting that infants apply a non-mentalistic system, the *teleological stance*, which interprets actions as processes that should realize goal-states efficiently (Gergely & Csibra, 2003; Gergely et al., 1995). They argue that such an implicit system precedes a functionally identical mentalistic system, namely the rationality principle. The authors thus propose a precursor to the richer conceptual system. The implicit system remains relatively complex, however. It is therefore relevant to point out that the rational–irrational path paradigm has a simpler, perceptual interpretation. The irrational conditions show that the paths, on their own, may well have little salience for the infants. Indeed, they look at novel and familiar paths for comparable durations. Rather, the removal of the obstacle on test trials in the rational conditions may well have a disruptive effect for infants. The familiar path without the obstacle may appear more novel than a new path without an obstacle, irrespective of the relative rationality of the path or of any perceived goal-directedness to the behaviour.

TOM IN INFANTS

ToM (Premack & Woodruff, 1978) is most likely the ultimate ability in humans' social cognitive toolkit. Equipped with ToM, it is possible to entertain recursive, *n*th order beliefs in *others'* minds (e.g., "I know that you know that I know"), which in turn give rise to the possibility of complex social interactions between individuals. Research into early precursors or indicators of ToM, apart from being interesting and important in its own right, could prove extremely valuable for early detection and intervention in autism, where ToM deficits are increasingly recognized as central (albeit not necessarily causal) features (Baron-Cohen, 2005; Hill & Frith, 2003; Joseph & Tager-Flusberg, 2004).

Although ToM has received substantial attention in childhood, there has been little work on ToM per se in infancy (although some of the work in the previous section on goal attribution might be construed as examining germinal ToM). Leslie recently argued that one reason for this paucity of infancy work on ToM is that a dogma in developmental psychology proposes that there is no ToM (as assessed by a standard, verbal *false belief* task) before the age of 4 years, thus that there is no innate ToM module to look for in infancy (Leslie, 2005).

The research from Onishi and Baillargeon (2005) was thus the first proper study of ToM in infants. In this study, 15-month-old infants were tested in a nonverbal implementation of the false belief (FB) task using a violation-of-expectation (VOE) paradigm. In a typical FB task (Wimmer & Perner, 1983), participants see a protagonist *P* observing an object being hidden in location *x*. Then *P* goes away and the object is moved to location *y*. *P* then returns and participants must say where they believe that *P* will search for the object. If participants can distinguish their belief (object is in *y*) from that of *P* (object is in *x*), and thus attribute different minds to others, they would answer that *P* would search in *x* rather than in *y*. In order to make this task appropriate for infants, Onishi and Baillargeon (2005) used looking-time measures for test events that either violated ToM beliefs or not.

Infants were first given three familiarization trials. On the first trial, a protagonist *P* picks up a toy and puts it in one of two boxes. On the second and third trial, *P* merely puts her hand in the box where the toy was hidden. These familiarization trials, shown in Figure 3, were followed by a single belief-induction trial. There were four such types of belief-induction trials, shown in Figure 4, and each infant saw only one. In one true belief (TB) induction trial, *P* observes the non-target box being moved left to right or right to left. The toy remains in the target box. In the other TB trial, *P* observes the toy moving from the initial box into the other target box. In both these TB trials, an infant with ToM would appreciate that *P* knows where the toy is currently hidden. In one false belief (FB) induction trial, *P* is absent as the toy moves from the initial box into the other box, while in the other FB trial, *P* observes the toy moving from the initial box to the other box but is absent when the toy moves back to the initial box. In both FB cases, an infant with ToM would anticipate that *P* would search for the toy in the wrong box. The belief induction trial was followed by the critical test trial. *P* merely put her hand in one of the boxes; counterbalanced across infants was whether or not this was the box in which the toy was hidden, which of the two boxes was used, and which of the four belief-induction

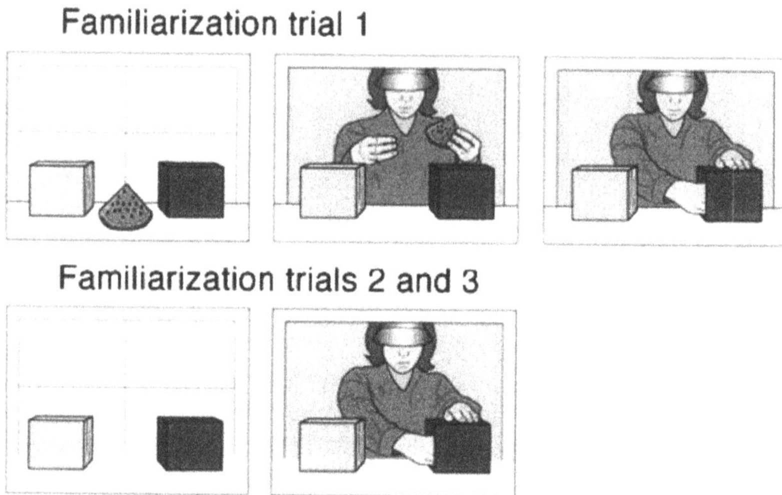

Figure 3. Familiarization trials used by Onishi and Baillargeon (2005) prior to belief-induction trials. The box shown in dark grey was green, whereas the light grey box was yellow. (From Onishi, K. H., & Baillargeon, R., 2005, Do 15-month-old infants understand false beliefs? *Science*, *308*, 255–258. Reprinted with permission from AAAS.)

trials was used. The hypothesis is that children should look longer at test events that violate their expectations (hence the VOE name). Predicted looking-time patterns would be inverted as a function of whether or not infants have ToM abilities.

Onishi and Baillargeon's (2005) results were consistent with suggestions that young children and infants' failures on verbal FB tasks stem from task demands rather than lack of ToM abilities. Indeed, 15-month-olds in their study looked longer when *P* made erroneous searches in the TB conditions, but looked longer when *P* made successful searches in FB conditions. In the words of these authors, "15-month-old infants … realize that others act on the basis of their beliefs and that these beliefs are representations that may or may not mirror reality" (Onishi & Baillargeon, 2005, p. 257). This suggests far more developed ToM skills than previous research with toddlers, and represents exciting news for researchers arguing, against dogma, for an innate ToM module (Leslie, 2005).

This initial work on false belief is not without problems, however. On the one hand, it suggests abilities in young infants that exceed abilities in toddlers. Indeed, anticipatory looking of 3-year-olds in FB tasks suggests some sensitivity to belief (Garnham & Ruffman, 2001), but not at the level shown in Onishi and Baillargeon's (2005) study. It is worth pointing out that many VOE studies suggest more advanced abilities in infants than toddlers (Keen, 2003), so the problem is not specific to this particular study. On the

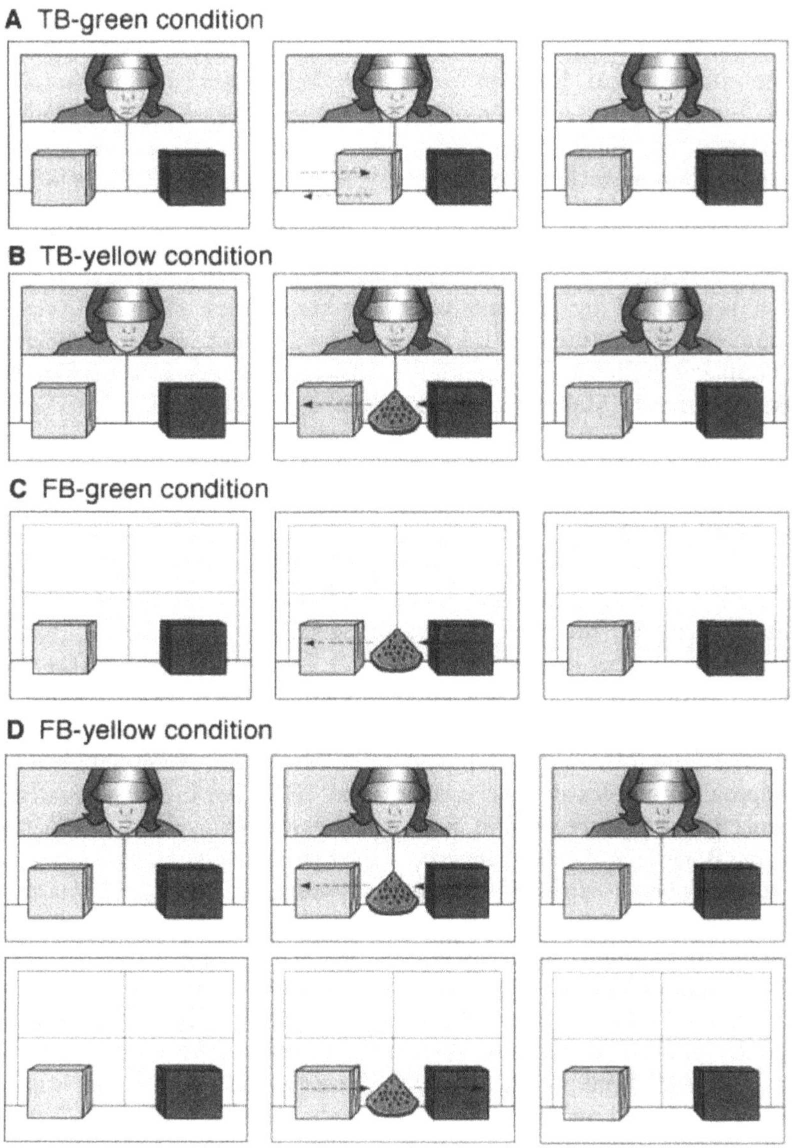

Figure 4. Belief-induction trials used by Onishi and Baillargeon (2005). Each infant saw only one such trial. (From Onishi, K. H., & Baillargeon, R., 2005, Do 15-month-old infants understand false beliefs? *Science*, *308*, 255–258. Reprinted with permission from AAAS.)

other hand, it is possible to explain the data from Onishi and Baillargeon without ascribing infants with beliefs about the protagonist. For example, infants could look longer at events that violate a triple-association between

P, the toy, and the box locations that specifies that *P* looks for toys where they were last seen (Perner & Ruffman, 2005; Ruffman & Perner, 2005).

Far more critical, however, are the methodological confounds in that work. First, infants were given only three familiarization trials with only the latter two of these being relatively simple. Looking times during familiarization were not reported, so it is not possible to assess whether infants habituated with such little training. However, it is well established in the habituation literature that novelty preferences (i.e., longer looking to novel items) are observed once initial learning is established (Fantz, 1964), which is affected by the complexity of the stimuli (Hunter, Ames, & Koopman, 1983). Moreover, it is common for infants to exhibit a preference for familiar stimuli early in habituation (Roder, Bushnell, & Sasseville, 2000; Rose, Gottfried, Melloy-Carminar, & Bridger, 1982). The problem of minimal familiarization in VOE paradigms has been receiving increased attention of late (Cohen, 2004; Schilling, 2000), as it severely compromises the interpretation of relative looking times (see also Haith, 1998; Malcuit, Pomerleau, & Lamarre, 1988).

Second, several variables distinguish the four belief-induction trials. These are: (1) object moved (toy vs box); (2) direction of movement (uni- vs bi-directional); (3) presence of protagonist (absent vs present vs partially present); (4) number of movements (1 vs 2); and (5) duration of trial (short vs long). Although the test trials are relatively straightforward, looking-time differences on those trials reflect differences from belief-induction trials that introduce multiple sources of perceptual variation. Analysing similarly perceptually complex designs used in other VOE work, using a statistical approach based on regression analysis of Event Set × Event Set factorial designs, Bogartz and colleagues have found that looking times on test trials are typically better explained by perceptual variables than by the conceptual knowledge under investigation (Bogartz & Shinskey, 1998; Bogartz, Shinskey, & Schilling, 2000; Bogartz et al., 1997). Until a similar analysis is carried out on the Onishi and Baillargeon (2005) design, the results are at best equivocal. It is not clear whether infants should exhibit a familiarity or a novelty preference, based on the limited number of familiarization trials, nor is it clear about which aspect of the single belief-induction trial this preference is based on, given the five perceptual variables that vary between the belief-induction events.

It remains the case that there are studies examining precursors of ToM that show a gradual emergence of abilities in infants. For instance, Legerstee and colleagues show how 6-month-old infants differentially process (assessed through looking times) targets of social interaction (people vs objects) as a function of the nature of the interaction carried out by a human actor (talking vs manipulating), and suggest that ToM is a gradually emerging ability (Legerstee, 2001; Legerstee, Barna, & DiAdamo, 2000), although the specific nature of what the precursors are remains debatable (Gergely, 2001). However, 7-month-olds gazed at an experimenter following an ambiguous event regardless of whether the experimenter attended to them or not, in contrast to 10-month-olds who gazed longer when the experimenter gazed back (Striano & Rochat, 2000). Recent behavioural and neural data suggest that similar abilities are measurable as early as 9 months (Striano, Chen, Cleveland, & Bradshaw, 2006; Striano, Reid, & Hoehl, 2006). This again suggests an emerging social ability. In an another study, 12-month-olds could be trained to follow both the gaze of persons and objects, but showed more temporally co-ordinated pointing, gazing and vocalizing when interacting with a person, relative to an object (Legerstee & Berillas, 2003). This shows how joint attention becomes social by the end of the first year, although the data do not require that we ascribe rich social abilities to infants. Rather, infants are shown to be aware of the attentional state of humans. Related research suggests that distinct joint-attention mechanisms emerge independently in the second year of life to support a nascent ToM (Slaughter & McConnell, 2003). Indeed, gaze following becomes increasing referential in this period (Dunphy-Lelii & Wellman, 2004). Similarly, Wellman and colleagues have shown how habituation to socially relevant events predict later ToM scores (Wellman et al., 2004), whereas Charman and his colleagues have shown that joint attention in infancy at 20 months is associated with ToM ability in early childhood (Charman et al., 2000) Overall, there is a wealth of research in infancy that supports social cognition as an emerging (rather than innately specified) ability, rooted in joint attention (Carpendale et al., 2004).

DISCUSSION

In this paper, we have identified many precursors to mature social cognitive abilities in infancy. However, we have failed to find compelling evidence for high-order abilities when we critically examined goal-directedness and ToM data. Rather, the majority of the literature seems to support a gradual emergence of social cognitive abilities (e.g., Nadel et al., 2004), whereby precursors seem to develop independently (even in the case of specific areas like joint attention; Slaughter & McConnell, 2003). It seems that early childhood is probably a better place to study high-order social cognitive skills. Yet some researchers have theoretically valid reasons to expect high-order skills in infancy (Leslie, 2005), and some of the infancy data may not be conclusive but remains consistent with high-order social cognition.

Povinelli and colleagues have argued that early social competence may well only exist to fool caregivers, and that the behaviours of infants have little to do with the social understanding found in children and adults (Povinelli et al., 2005). Many precursors, in fact, rely on different neural structures to those found in adults (Johnson, 1990; Povinelli et al., 2005). Specifically, Povinelli and colleagues (2005) suggest that the appearance of social competence (rather than actual competence) helps to solidify the bond between infant and caregivers, resulting in the latter increasing the investment in the former, with obvious evolutionary advantages. In other words, a baby that quickly appears to be socially attuned to its caregivers and immediate social group (through social smiling, gaze following, pointing, etc.) would be deemed more worthy of the sort of attention that would enhance its survival. Povinelli et al. (2005) further argue that the early precursors of social behaviour may well be structurally equivalent to later behaviours yet may not, in fact, be causal precursors. However, the precursors would help bootstrap the infant in social interactions from which to acquire the mature functions.

This idea is consistent with primate work showing that conflict over investment (infants want more, parents want less) is an important issue (Maestripieri, 2002). Given that differences in social cognition between humans and primates are arguably more qualitative than quantitative (Tomasello et al., 2005), consistency with comparative data is likely desirable. We will thus work with the assumption that there were adaptive reasons for infants to display socially contingent behaviours, but that there were no reasons for these behaviours to involve actual social understanding. In fact, the emergence of social cognition was likely in order to enable humans to make better use of existing abilities, and not to provide for a new range of behaviours (Povinelli & Prince, 1998). If fancy abilities like goal-attribution and ToM are only made possible by the simpler functions selected through evolution (rather than being selected themselves), it is unlikely we will find evidence for those higher order, side-effect functions early in infancy, prior to the deployment and integration of precursor functions.

Research on social cognition in infancy may well want to carry on with bottom-up work that identifies precursors and examine how they combine into complex abilities (Charman et al., 2000; Gergely, 2001; Legerstee et al., 2000; Nadel et al., 2004). There is overwhelming evidence for these abilities in infants, and the holy grail in this area may well be to chart how these distinct abilities functionally integrate to produce socially competent individuals.

Top-down studies that search for early indicators of complex skills may not prove a fruitful avenue. On the one hand, the skills may not be there to begin with (Povinelli et al., 2005). And if they are, they may not be the same skills as used by older children and adults and rely on entirely different neural circuits (Johnson, 1990), in which case ascribing early competence would be partly misleading. On the other hand, the commonly used VOE paradigm suffers from methodological issues that complicate the interpretation of data—data for which there are usually alternative interpretations

(Haith, 1998). The moment that test trials are perceptually distinct (and, by definition, they must be, regardless of the conceptual knowledge under scrutiny), there usually are perceptual interpretations. Based on the evidence reviewed in this paper, we suggest that the most fruitful approach to social cognition in infancy has been bottom-up work that identifies the emergence of abilities, and that such approaches are likely to remain the most fruitful, with potentially useful guidance from the neurosciences (e.g., Aslin & Fiser, 2005; Sirois & Mareschal, 2002; Striano & Reid, 2006).

REFERENCES

Adolphs, R. (2003). Cognitive neuroscience of human social behaviour. *Nature Reviews Neuroscience*, *4*(3), 165–178.

Anisfeld, M., Turkewitz, G., Rose, S. A., Rosenberg, F. R., Sheiber, F. J., Couturier-Fagan, D. A., et al. (2001). No compelling evidence that newborns imitate oral gestures. *Infancy*, *2*(1), 111–122.

Aslin, R. N., & Fiser, J. (2005). Methodological challenges for understanding cognitive development in infants. *Trends in Cognitive Sciences*, *9*(3), 92–98.

Baron-Cohen, S. (2005). Autism and the origins of social neuroscience. In A. Easton & N. J. Emery (Eds.), *The cognitive neuroscience of social behaviour* (pp. 239–255). New York: Psychology Press.

Bogartz, R. S., & Shinskey, J. L. (1998). On perception of a partially occluded object in 6-month-olds. *Cognitive Development*, *13*(2), 141–163.

Bogartz, R. S., Shinskey, J. L., & Schilling, T. H. (2000). Object permanence in five-and-a half-month-old infants? *Infancy*, *1*(4), 403–428.

Bogartz, R. S., Shinskey, J. L., & Speaker, C. J. (1997). Interpreting infant looking: The event set * event set design. *Developmental Psychology*, *33*(3), 408–422.

Butterworth, G., & Jarrett, N. (1991). What minds have in common is space: Spatial mechanisms serving joint visual attention in infancy. *British Journal of Developmental Psychology*, *9*(1), 55–72.

Carpendale, J. I. M., Lewis, C., Muller, U., & Racine, T. P. (2004). Constructing perspectives in the social making of minds. *Interaction Studies: Social Behaviour and Communication in Biological and Artificial Systems*, *6*(3), 341–358.

Charman, T., Baron-Cohen, S., Swettenham, J., Baird, G., Cox, A., & Drew, A. (2000). Testing joint attention, imitation, and play as infancy precursors to language and theory of mind. *Cognitive Development*, *15*(4), 481–498.

Chen, X., Reid, V., & Striano, T. (2006). Oral exploration and reaching toward social and non-social objects in two-, four-, and six-month-old infants. *European Journal of Developmental Psychology*, *3*(1), 1–12.

Cohen, L. B. (2004). Uses and misuses of habituation and related preference paradigms. *Infant and Child Development*, *13*(4), 349–352.

Csibra, G., Gergely, G., Biro, S., Koos, O., & Brockbank, M. (1999). Goal attribution without agency cues: The perception of "pure reason" in infancy. *Cognition*, *72*(3), 237–267.

Dunphy-Lelii, S., & Wellman, H. M. (2004). Infants' understanding of occlusion of others' line-of-sight: Implications for an emerging theory of mind. *European Journal of Developmental Psychology*, *1*(1), 49–66.

Emde, R. N., & Koenig, K. L. (1969). Neonatal smiling and rapid eye movement states. *Journal of the American Academy of Child Psychiatry*, *8*(1), 57–67.

Fantz, R. L. (1964). Visual experience in infants: Decreased attention to familiar patterns relative to novel ones. *Science*, *146*(3644), 668–670.

Garnham, W. A., & Ruffman, T. (2001). Doesn't see, doesn't know: Is anticipatory looking really related to understanding or belief? *Developmental Science*, *4*(1), 94–100.

Gergely, G. (2001). Is early differentiation of human behavior a precursor to the 1-year-old's understanding of intentional action? Comment on Legerstee, Barna, and DiAdamo (2000). *Developmental Psychology*, *37*(5), 579–582.

Gergely, G., & Csibra, G. (2003). Teleological reasoning in infancy: The naive theory of rational action. *Trends in Cognitive Sciences*, *7*(7), 287–292.

Gergely, G., Nadasdy, Z., Csibra, G., & Biro, S. (1995). Taking the intentional stance at 12 months of age. *Cognition*, *56*(2), 165–193.

Goren, C. C., Sarty, M., & Wu, P. Y. (1975). Visual following and pattern discrimination of face-like stimuli by newborn infants. *Pediatrics*, *56*(4), 544–549.

Hains, S. M. J., & Muir, D. W. (1996). Infant sensitivity to adult eye direction. *Child Development*, *67*(5), 1940–1951.

Haith, M. M. (1998). Who put the cog in infant cognition? Is rich interpretation too costly? *Infant Behavior & Development*, *21*(2), 167–179.

Hill, E. L., & Frith, U. (2003). Understanding autism: Insights from mind and brain. In U. Frith & E. L. Hill (Eds.), *Autism: Mind and brain* (pp. 1–19). Oxford, UK: Oxford University Press.

Hunter, M. A., Ames, E. W., & Koopman, R. (1983). Effects of stimulus complexity and familiarization time on infant preferences for novel and familiar stimuli. *Developmental Psychology*, *19*(3), 338–352.

Johnson, M. H. (1990). Cortical maturation and the development of visual attention in early infancy. *Journal of Cognitive Neuroscience*, *2*, 81–95.

Johnson, M. H., Dziurawiec, S., Ellis, H., & Morton, J. (1991). Newborns' preferential tracking of face-like stimuli and its subsequent decline. *Cognition*, *40*(1–2), 1–19.

Jones, S. S. (1996). Imitation or exploration? Young infants' matching of adults' oral gestures. *Child Development*, *67*(5), 1952–1969.

Joseph, R. M., & Tager-Flusberg, H. (2004). The relationship of theory of mind and executive functions to symptom type and severity in children with autism. *Development and Psychopathology*, *16*(1), 137–155.

Keen, R. (2003). Representation of objects and events: Why do infants look so smart and toddlers look so dumb? *Current Directions in Psychological Science*, *12*(3), 79–83.

Legerstee, M. (2001). Six-month-old infants rely on explanatory inference when relating communication to people and manipulatory actions to inanimate objects: Reply to Gergely (2001). *Developmental Psychology*, *37*(5), 583–586.

Legerstee, M., Barna, J., & DiAdamo, C. (2000). Precursors to the development of intention at 6 months: Understanding people and their actions. *Developmental Psychology*, *36*(5), 627–634.

Legerstee, M., & Berillas, Y. (2003). Sharing attention and pointing to objects at 12 months: Is the intentional stance implied? *Cognitive Development*, *18*(1), 91–110.

Leslie, A. M. (2005). Developmental parallels in understanding minds and bodies. *Trends in Cognitive Sciences*, *9*(10), 459–462.

Maestripieri, D. (2002). Parent–offspring conflict in primates. *International Journal of Primatology*, *23*(4), 923–951.

Malcuit, G., Pomerleau, A., & Lamarre, G. (1988). Habituation, visual fixation and cognitive activity in infants: A critical analysis and attempt at a new formulation. *Cahiers de Psychologie Cognitive*, *8*(5), 415–440.

Meltzoff, A. N., & Moore, M. K. (1977). Imitation of facial and manual gestures by human neonates. *Science*, *198*(4312), 75–78.

Morton, J., & Johnson, M. H. (1991). CONSPEC and CONLERN: A two-process theory of infant face recognition. *Psychological Review, 98*(2), 164–181.

Myowa-Yamakoshi, M., Yamaguchi, M. K., Tomonaga, M., Tanaka, M., & Matsuzawa, T. (2005). Development of face recognition in infant chimpanzees (*Pan troglodytes*). *Cognitive Development, 20*(1), 49–63.

Nadel, J., Prepin, K., & Okanda, M. (2004). Experiencing contingency and agency: First step toward self-understanding in making a mind? *Interaction Studies: Social Behaviour and Communication in Biological and Artificial Systems, 6*(3), 447–462.

Onishi, K. H., & Baillargeon, R. (2005). Do 15-month-old infants understand false beliefs? *Science, 308*(5719), 255–258.

Perner, J., & Ruffman, T. (2005). Infants' insight into the mind: How deep? *Science, 308*(5719), 214–216.

Povinelli, D. J., & Prince, C. G. (1998). When self met other. In M. D. Ferrari & R. J. Sternberg (Eds.), *Self-awareness: Its nature and development* (pp. 37–107). New York: Guilford Press.

Povinelli, D. J., Prince, C. G., & Preuss, T. M. (2005). Parent–offspring conflict and the development of social understanding. In P. Carruthers, S. Laurence, & S. Stich (Eds.), *The innate mind: Structure and contents* (pp. 239–253). Oxford, UK: Oxford University Press.

Premack, D., & Woodruff, G. (1978). Does the chimpanzee have a theory of mind. *Behavioral and Brain Sciences, 1*(4), 515–526.

Roder, B. J., Bushnell, E. W., & Sasseville, A. M. (2000). Infants' preferences for familiarity and novelty during the course of visual processing. *Infancy, 1*(4), 491–507.

Rose, S. A., Gottfried, A. W., Melloy-Carminar, P., & Bridger, W. H. (1982). Familiarity and novelty preferences in infant recognition memory: Implications for information processing. *Developmental Psychology, 18*(5), 704–713.

Ruffman, T., & Perner, J. (2005). Do infants really understand false belief? *Trends in Cognitive Sciences, 9*(10), 462–463.

Scaife, M., & Bruner, J. S. (1975). The capacity for joint visual attention in the infant. *Nature, 253*(5489), 265–266.

Schilling, T. H. (2000). Infants' looking at possible and impossible screen rotations: The role of familiarization. *Infancy, 1*(4), 389–402.

Sirois, S., & Mareschal, D. (2002). Models of habituation in infancy. *Trends in Cognitive Sciences, 6*(7), 293–298.

Slaughter, V., & McConnell, D. (2003). Emergence of joint attention: Relationships between gaze following, social referencing, imitation, and naming in infancy. *Journal of Genetic Psychology, 164*(1), 54–71.

Sodian, B., Schoeppner, B., & Metz, U. (2004). Do infants apply the principle of rational action to human agents? *Infant Behavior and Development, 27*(1), 31– 41.

Sommerville, J. A., & Woodward, A. L. (2005). Pulling out the intentional structure of action: The relation between action processing and action production in infancy. *Cognition, 95*(1), 1–30.

Spelke, E. S. (1999). Innateness, learning and the development of object representation. *Developmental Science, 2*(2), 145–148.

Striano, T., Chen, X., Cleveland, A., & Bradshaw, S. (2006). Joint attention social cues influence infant learning. *European Journal of Developmental Psychology, 3*(3), 289–299.

Striano, T., & Reid, V. M. (2006). Social cognition in the first year. *Trends in Cognitive Sciences, 10*(10), 471–476.

Striano, T., Reid, V. M., & Hoehl, S. (2006). Neural mechanisms of joint attention in infancy. *European Journal of Neuroscience, 23*(10), 2819–2823.

Striano, T., & Rochat, P. (2000). Emergence of selective social referencing in infancy. *Infancy, 1*(2), 253–264.

Tomasello, M. (2003). *Constructing a language: A usage-based theory of language acquisition*. Cambridge, MA: Harvard University Press.

Tomasello, M., Carpenter, M., Call, J., Behne, T., & Moll, H. (2005). Understanding and sharing intentions: The origins of cultural cognition. *Behavioral and Brain Sciences*, *28*(5), 675–735.

Tomonaga, M., Tanaka, M., Matsuzawa, T., Myowa-Yamakoshi, M., Kosugi, D., Mizuno, Y. et al. (2004). Development of social cognition in infant chimpanzees (*Pan troglodytes*): Face recognition, smiling, gaze, and the lack of triadic interactions. *Japanese Psychological Research*, *46*(3), 227–235.

Watson, J. S. (1972). Smiling, cooing, and "the game". *Merrill-Palmer Quarterly*, *18*(4), 323–339.

Wellman, H. M., Phillips, A. T., Dunphy-Lelii, S., & LaLonde, N. (2004). Infant social attention predicts preschool social cognition. *Developmental Science*, *7*(3), 283–288.

Wimmer, H., & Perner, J. (1983). Beliefs about beliefs: Representation and constraining function of wrong beliefs in young children's understanding of deception. *Cognition*, *13*(1), 103–128.

Woodward, A. L. (1998). Infants selectively encode the goal object of an actor's reach. *Cognition*, *69*(1), 1–34.

Woodward, A. L. (1999). Infants' ability to distinguish between purposeful and non-purposeful behaviors. *Infant Behavior & Development*, *22*(2), 145–160.

EUROPEAN JOURNAL OF DEVELOPMENTAL PSYCHOLOGY
2007, 4 (1), 65–79

Object processing during a joint gaze following task

Carolin Theuring
Max-Planck Institute for Human Cognitive and Brain Sciences, Munich, Germany

Gustaf Gredebäck
University of Oslo, Norway

Petra Hauf
St. Francis Xavier University, Antigonish, NS, Canada

To investigate object processing in a gaze following task, 12-month-old infants were presented with 4 movies in which a female model turned and looked at one of two objects. This was followed by 2 test trials showing the two objects alone without the model. Eye movements were recorded with a Tobii-1750 eye tracker. Infants reliably followed gaze and displayed longer looking times towards the attended object when the model was present. During the first test trial infants displayed a brief novelty preference for the unattended object. These findings suggest that enhanced object processing is a temporarily restricted phenomenon that has little effect on 12-month-old infants' long-term interaction with the environment.

Gaze following is an essential element of joint visual attention and an important ingredient of the development of early social cognition (Moore & Corkum, 1994; Tomasello, 1999). It enables an individual to obtain useful information about his/her surrounding by observing others' behaviour. This ability is not restricted to humans but occurs in numerous other species, e.g., great apes or domestic dogs (e.g., Bräuer, Call, & Tomasello, 2005; Hare, Call, & Tomasello, 1999). Typically, gaze following has been studied in "live" social situations, where an adult initially establishes eye contact with the infant and thereafter turns to and fixates one of several objects. Infants'

Correspondence should be addressed to Gustaf Gredebäck, The Cognitive Developmental Research Unit, Department of Psychology, University of Oslo, Box 1094, Blindern, 0317 Oslo, Norway. E-mail: gustaf.gredeback@psykologi.uio.no

The current paper was supported by grant 174038 from the Norwegian Directorate for Children, Youth, and Family Affairs.

DOI: 10.1080/17405620601051246

tendency to follow others gaze is typically measured by relating the infants first eye turn to the direction of the adults attention (D'Entremont, Hains, & Muir, 1997; Hood, Willen, & Driver, 1998; Johnson, Slaughter, & Carey, 1998; Moore & Corkum, 1998; Scaife & Bruner, 1975) or by comparing looking durations towards attended and unattended locations (Reid & Striano, 2005; von Hofsten, Dahlström, & Fredriksson, 2005).

Some authors argue that infants can follow others' gaze direction from 6 months of age (e.g., Butterworth, & Cochran, 1980; D'Entremont et al., 1997; Morales, Mundy, & Rojas, 1998). Others have not found evidence of gaze following until infants are between 9 and 12 months of age (Corkum & Moore, 1998; Flom, Deák, Phill, & Pick, 2004; Moore & Corkum, 1998; Morissette, Ricard, & Gouin Décarie, 1995). The exact onset of this ability might still be debated. However, it appears safe to say that infants at 12 months of age follow others' gaze; responding to the behavioural manifestations of others' psychological orientations (Moore & Corkum, 1994; see also Johnson et al., 1998; Woodward, 2003).

Despite this, little is known about how infants at this age process the object of others' attention. It is tempting to assume that an infant, by following the gaze of another person to an object, naturally also understands the psychological relationship between the person and the attended object, as if saying: "this specific thing was interesting for this person", but, de facto, little is known about the development of the actual function of gaze following beyond target localization. This study aimed to increase our understanding of how infants' object processing is influenced by the direction of others' gaze.

In a study by Reid, Striano, Kaufman, and Johnson (2004), 4-month-old infants were presented with a frontal face and one object either to the left or to the right side; these events were presented on a video screen. After one second the eyes rotated either towards (cued) or away (non-cued) from the object and fixated that location for one additional second. Following this period the face disappeared and the previously presented object appeared in its place. Throughout the experiment EEG was recorded. The results demonstrated lower peak amplitudes for slow wave ERPs in response to previously cued as opposed to non-cued objects. This effect was interpreted as a novelty preference to non-cued objects, resulting from enhanced object processing to the attended (cued) compared to the unattended (non-cued) object.

In a different experiment by Reid and Striano (2005) 4-month-olds were similarly presented with an adult face, but this time with two objects present, one to either side of the face. The adult's eyes were initially directed forward, shifting to one side and fixating one of the objects after one second. After a brief intermission the two objects were presented without the face. During this later phase infants' looking durations to each of the two objects were recorded. Infants looked reliably longer at the non-cued compared to the cued object; this novelty preference indicates that infants were influenced by the model's gaze shift and that the non-cued object was more interesting than the object previously attended by the adult face. This result again demonstrates an enhanced object processing as a function of others' gaze direction.

These studies clearly demonstrate that infants at 4 months of age are sensitive to others' gaze direction. They are, however, unable to inform us about what impact this enhanced object processing has on infants' future interaction with the attended object for two reasons. First of all, both studies were performed on an age group that is not frequently reported to follow others' gaze direction. Reid et al. (2004) clearly state that: "no infants overtly followed the gaze to the object location", suggesting that the reported effects are not the result of shifts in overt attention but rather result from subtle shifts in covert attention without behavioural correlates. A lack of eye movements is obviously a prerequisite of high quality ERP data (reducing the noise level by minimizing eye movements); however, this gives us no indication that the studied infants could follow gaze direction. In another study, Reid and Striano (2005) did not report whether infants follow the model's gaze direction or not.

In addition, it is still unclear what is meant by "enhanced object processing". One interpretation is that infants simply follow the model's gaze direction without attributing any meaning to the model's behaviour. In this case infants' preference for non-attended objects should appear as a temporarily restricted novelty preference with little bearing on infants' long-term interaction with the attended object. Another interpretation is that infants' attribute some kind of meaning to the attended object, perhaps infants understand the relationship between the model's attention and the object and, as a consequence thereof, differentiate this object from the other object over time.

If one wishes to gain a better understanding of how others' gaze direction influences infants' object processing it is important to focus on an age group that has a well-documented ability to follow others' gaze direction and to use a paradigm with a high spatial-temporal resolution that allows us to evaluate the temporal restraints of infants' object processing and whether infants follow the model's gaze. The current study attempts to answer these questions by measuring gaze following and object processing in 12-month-old infants using high-resolution eye-tracking technology.

METHOD

Participants

Sixteen 12-month-old healthy, full-term infants (mean age 11 months and 28 days, $SD = 2$ days) participated in this study. Four infants were eliminated because of refusal to remain seated or because of technical problems. Participants were contacted by mail based on birth records. As compensation for their participation each family received either two movie tickets or a CD voucher with a total value of 15 €.

Stimuli and apparatus

Gaze was measured using a Tobii 1750 near infrared eye tracker with an infant add-on (Tobii Technology; www.Tobii.se). The system records the reflection of near infrared light in the pupil and cornea of both eyes at 50 Hz (accuracy = 0.5 degrees, spatial resolution = 0.25 degrees) as participants watch an integrated 17-inch monitor. During calibration infants were presented with a looming and sounding blue and white sphere (extended diameter = 3.3 degrees; Gredebäck & von Hofsten, 2004). The calibration stimulus could be briefly exchanged for an attention-grabbing movie (horizontal and vertical extension = 5.7 degrees) if infants temporarily looked away from the calibration stimulus.

The stimuli set consisted of 30 movies. Twenty included a female model that shifted her gaze (head and eyes) to one of two toys placed on either side of the model (Figure 1A). Each movie included two toys randomly selected from a set of 5 unique toy pairs. The toy pairs were counterbalanced with regards to which toy the model attended and their respective locations, which equal $5 \times 2 \times 2$ variations. Ten additional movies without the model were also included (Figure 1B). Again the five toy pairs were counterbalanced for location, which equal 5×2 variations.

Movies that included the model lasted on average for 13 seconds. Each movie started with a 5-second period during which the model looked down at the table in front of her with the two toys visible on either side (see Figure 1A1). After 5 seconds the model moved her face upwards and fixated straight ahead (see Figure 1A2 for endpoint of upwards motion), this movement lasted for 1.5 seconds. During these 6.5 seconds the model had not yet attended to either toy. This part is referred to as the Baseline block. The following 1.5 seconds involved a sideways downwards movement of the model's head and eyes towards one of the toys, accompanied by a smile. The movie ended with a 5-second interval in which the model kept fixating the toy. These last 6.5 seconds of the sequence are referred to as the Gaze Direction block (see Figure 1A3). The purpose of the current study was to investigate the depth of infants' object processing during a joint gaze following task. The stimulus material was therefore designed to simulate the natural interaction between an infant and an adult. As such, the model shifted her gaze and directed positive regard to a near object. For the same purpose the action was presented over the extended period of 13 seconds altogether. The infants should have been given time to encode and react to

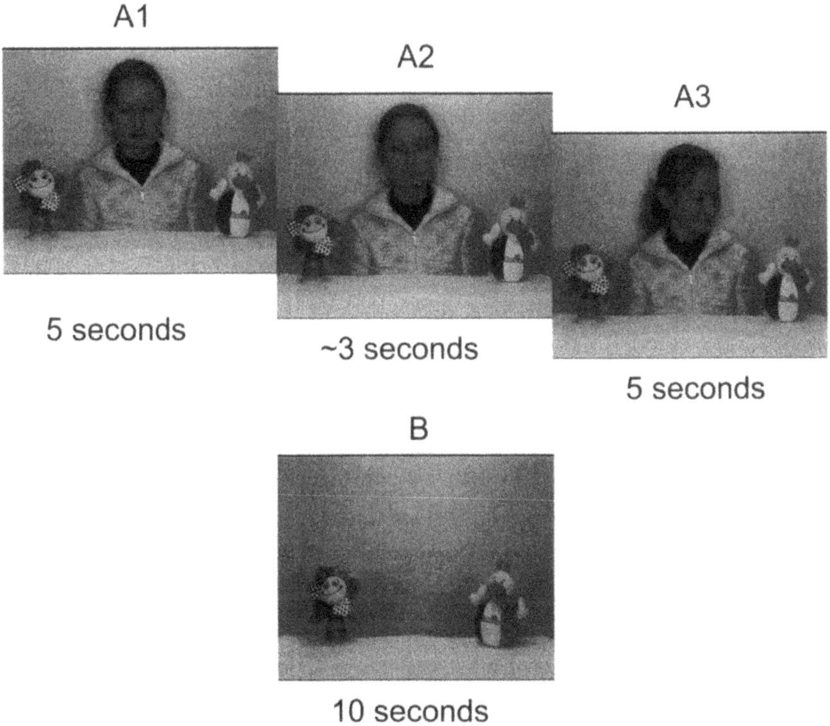

Figure 1. Timeline and sample stimuli with the model present (A) and during the Test block (B). The Baseline includes the first 5 seconds (A1) and the duration when the model looks up (up to the frame depicted in A2). The Gaze Direction block starts when the model indicates the direction of gaze (following the frame depicted in A2) and ends with the termination of the movie (A3).

the full situation, as if in any playful situation with an adult. Movies that did not include a model lasted for 10 seconds. In these movies the two objects were displayed on their own (Figure 1B).

Procedure

Infants were seated in a safety car seat and placed on their parent's lap with their eyes about 60 cm from the eye tracker. During calibration the looming stimulus described above was presented at nine different locations in a random order. If the infant's attention was drawn to other parts of the visual field during this procedure the experimenter exchanged the calibration stimulus for an alternative attention-grabbing movie at the current location. If any points were unsuccessfully calibrated these points were recalibrated.

Infants were always presented with four trials that included the model. During these presentations the model always attended to the same toy, but its location changed between presentations according to an ABBA design. For example, the attended toy might first appear to the left, followed by two movies in which the toy appeared to the right, and a final movie in which the attended toy appeared to the left. These presentations were followed by two test trials in which the toys appeared on their own, again at switched locations. Each infant was presented with one of two presentation orders ABBA – BA or BAAB – AB.

This presentation order was necessary to ensure the infants would interpret the model's behaviour as object directed and not as directed to a particular side of their visual field. In addition, reversing the location of the objects between the last trial with the model and the first test trials (and between the first and second test trial) ensured that infants' paid attention to the objects and not just the disappearance of the model.

After the experiment parents were given the opportunity to look at a replay of the stimuli that included the infants' gaze. In general each family spent 15 to 20 minutes in the lab.

Data reduction

Infants had to fixate the model's face and then shift their gaze to one of the toys after the model started moving her head on at least three trials to be included in the analysis. These infants further fixated each object location at least once during the Gaze Direction block. Gaze data were transformed to fixation data with a spatial-temporal filter covering 200 ms and 50 pixels (approximately 1 visual degree) in ClearView (Tobii). All analyses were performed using a custom-made analysis program in Matlab (Mathworks).

Data from each trial that included the model were separated into a Baseline block, including the beginning of each trial until the model had raised her head, and a Gaze Direction block, including the entire head movement and the model's subsequent fixation on an object. Data from the Test block were analysed as a whole. Each trial of these blocks was analysed separately. The blocks were used in an area-of-interest (AOI) analysis including only fixations within any one of three equally sized areas, covering face, left toy, and right toy. These analyses calculated effects in two ways: according to the location of each fixation, and with respect to the AOIs covering the attended or unattended toy (see Figure 2 for approximate size and location of AOIs). Note that the AOI analysis included more detailed information by separating the face from the toys and excluding fixations at other parts of the screen than typically used preferential looking paradigms for which the screen would have been divided into left and right sections

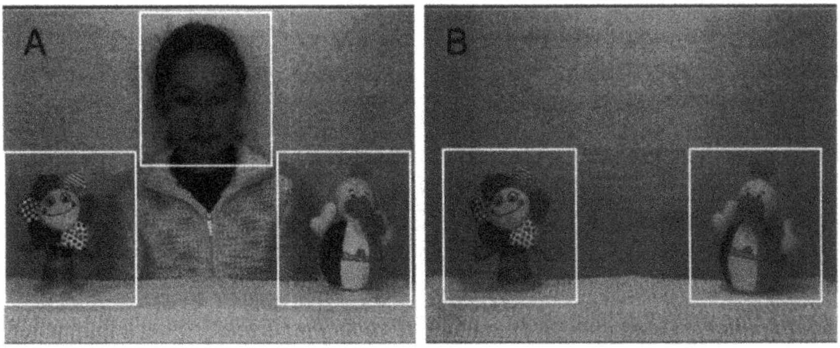

Figure 2. White squares represent AOIs covering the face and any of the two toys during trials with the model present (A) and during test trials (B). AOI squares do not represent the exact size used for analysis.

only. Observe that during test trials AOI analysis was based on the AOIs covering the attended or unattended toy (see Figure 2B).

As infants differ in overall fixation duration, proportional fixation duration was calculated (attended = fixation duration attended/fixation duration attended + fixation duration unattended; unattended = fixation duration unattended/fixation duration attended + fixation duration unattended). Only this proportional fixation duration is reported in the result section below.

Focus was also directed at the first fixations and individual gaze shifts. Infants' first fixation of the model's face and the two toys during the Baseline block and the Gaze Direction block was registered (after infants had fixated the model's face for at least 200 ms during this block) together with the duration of this fixation. During Baseline and Gaze Direction blocks the fixated target was registered and whether or not the attended target was the one being fixated. Additionally, infants' first gaze shift from the model's face to a toy (as defined by the AOIs) during the Gaze Direction block was registered. During the Test block infants' proportional fixation duration was analysed with respect to the AOIs covering the two toys (see Figure 2B) as well as the first fixation of a toy. Also the first fixated toy was included.

In addition, a difference score (DS; cf. Corkum & Moore, 1998; Moore & Corkum, 1998) was calculated for each infant in order to reliably investigate gaze following during the Gaze Direction block. This DS was determined by the number of trials where the infants' first gaze shifted from the face to the attended toy, minus the number of trials where infants went to the unattended toy first. DS could thus vary from +4 (shifting in all trials to the attended toy) to −4 (shifting in all trials to the unattended toy).

RESULTS

Baseline block

The mean fixation duration during the four Baseline trials within all three AOIs equalled 4405 ms ($SE = 202$ ms). More time was spent looking at the face ($M = 49.48\%$, $SE = 2.64\%$) than at either toy ($M_{\text{left}} = 20.52\%$, $SE = 2.17\%$ and $M_{\text{right}} = 30.00\%$, $SE = 2.92\%$), $F(2, 45) = 27.613$, $p = .000$, $\eta^2 = .551$. Separated t-tests differentiated the face from both the left toy, $t(46) = 7.505$, $p = .0000$, as well as from the right toy, $t(46) = 3.794$, $p = .0004$, which additionally differed from each other, $t(46) = 2.146$, $p = .037$. Note that even though infants spent more time looking at the right AOI than at the left AOI there were no significant differences between the AOI that later would be the attended (45.8%, $SE = 4.7\%$) and the unattended (54.2%, $SE = 4.7\%$) AOI, $t(47) = 0.887$, $p = .380$ (see Figure 3).

Gaze Direction block

During the Gaze Direction block 4625 ms ($SE = 259$ ms) was spent fixating the three AOIs on average. More time was spent fixating the face ($M = 59.11\%$, $SE = 3.04\%$) than either the left ($M = 19.7\%$, $SE = 2.8\%$) or the right ($M = 21.2\%$, $SE = 2.5\%$) toy, $F(2, 45) = 34.806$, $p = .000$, $\eta^2 = .607$. Post hoc tests differentiated the face from both the left, $t(46) = 7.609$, $p = .000$, as well as from the right toy, $t(46) = 7.628$, $p = .000$, which did not differ ($p = .570$; see Figure 3). In contrast to the Baseline block, now the attended toy was fixated to a higher degree ($M = 67.5\%$, $SE = 4.5\%$) than the unattended toy ($M = 32.5\%$, $SE = 4.5\%$), $t(43) = 3.797$, $p = .0005$.

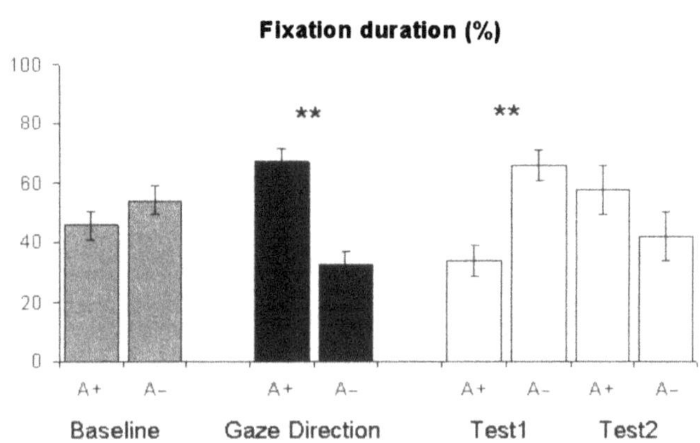

Figure 3. Average proportional fixation durations to the attended (A+) and unattended (A−) toy, based on AOI, in Baseline (B) and Gaze Direction (GD) blocks and the two test trials. Error bars indicate standard error and ** depict significant differences.

Test block

In total infants spent 6588 ms ($SE = 487$ ms) fixating the two AOIs during the Test block. Thereby infants looked equally long at the right ($M = 50.88\%$, $SE = 5.47\%$) and the left ($M = 49.12\%$, $SE = 5.47\%$) toy, $t(23) = 0.164$, $p = .871$. The proportional fixation of the toys during the Test block was analysed by a 2×2 analysis of variance (ANOVA) with the within-subject factors Test (trial 1 and trial 2) and Toy (attended or unattended). The analysis yielded a marginally significant test trial × toy interaction, $F(1, 11) = 3.981$, $p = .071$, $\eta^2 = .266$, but no significant main effects ($ps > .189$). Even though infants' overall fixation times did not differ between the attended toy ($M = 45.8\%$, $SE = 5.4$) and the unattended ($M = 54.2\%$, $SE = 5.4$) toy during the entire Test block, $t(23) = 0.795$, $p = .435$, post hoc tests differentiated the fixation duration of the first test trial from the fixation duration of the second test trial (see Figure 3). The previously unattended toy was fixated to a higher degree ($M = 66.2\%$, $SE = 5.4\%$) than the previously attended toy ($M = 33.8\%$, $SE = 5.4\%$) during the first of two test trials, $t(11) = 3.166$, $p = .009$. However, during the second test trial infants fixated both toys equally long—previously unattended toy: $M = 42.2\%$, $SE = 8.4\%$; previously attended toy: $M = 57.8\%$, $SE = 8.4\%$; $t(11) = 0.971$, $p = .352$. In addition, the fixation duration during the first test trial did not correlate with the fixation duration during the Gaze Direction block, $r_{xy} = .103$, $p = .750$.

The analysis of the fixation duration demonstrated that infants spent a different amount of time looking at the two toys during both the Gaze Direction block and the Test block. Interestingly, infants showed no preference at all during the Baseline block. An especially detailed analysis was conducted covering the first fixation and the order of presentation.

Analysis of first gaze shift and first fixation

The first gaze shift from the model's face to a toy during the Gaze Direction block was analysed separately. Infants' first gaze shifts were directed to the attended toy in 38 of 46 trials, $\chi^2\,(1) = 19.565$, $p = .000$, with an averaged DS of 2.17 ($SE = 0.48$), indicating that infants were reliably following the model's gaze. This first gaze shift did not correlate with the fixation duration during the first test trial, $r = .089$, $p = .783$. The first fixation of a toy was analysed by a 3×2 ANOVA with the within-subject factors Block (baseline, gaze direction, and test) and Toy (attended or unattended). The analysis yielded a significant block × toy interaction, $F(2, 10) = 6.297$, $p = .017$, $\eta^2 = .557$, but no significant main effects ($ps > .312$), indicating that the infants' first fixations to the attended toy differed among the blocks; see Figure 4 for the percentage of first fixation on the toys. Accordingly,

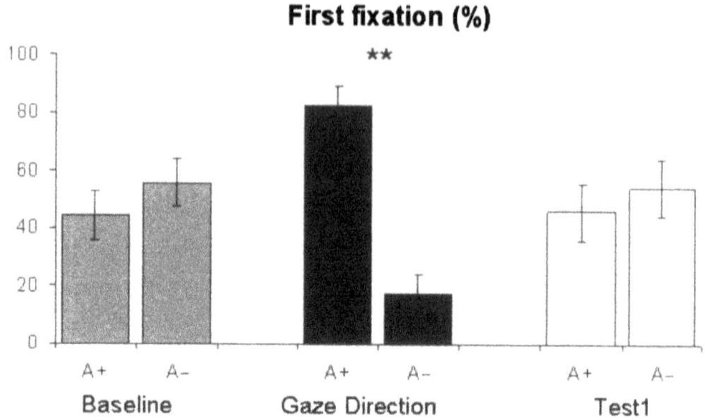

Figure 4. Average percentage scores of the first saccade directed to the attended (A+) and unattended (A−) target based on AOI, in Baseline (B), Gaze Direction (GD) and Test blocks. Error bars indicate standard error and ** depict significant differences.

separated *t*-tests revealed that the first fixation was significantly directed to the attended toy during the Gaze Direction block ($M = 82.7\%$, $SE = 6.8\%$), $t(11) = 5.011$, $p = .0004$, whereas no differences occurred in the first fixation between the attended toy ($M = 44.4\%$, $SE = 8.5\%$) and the unattended toy ($M = 55.6\%$, $SE = 8.5\%$) during the Baseline block, $t(11) = 0.689$, $p = .505$, and the Test block, attended toy: $M = 45.8\%$, $SE = 10.1\%$; unattended toy: $M = 54.2\%$, $SE = 10.1\%$, $t(11) = 0.432$, $p = .674$. In addition, the percentage of first fixation directed to the left toy was not significantly different from the percentage of first fixation directed to the right toy during all blocks (all *ps* $> .522$).

Analysis of the presentation order

Each infant was presented with four trials where the model always attended to the same toy, but its location was changed between trials according to an ABBA design (cf. procedure). The subsequent test trial without the model presented the toys again in changed location (B). In order to investigate the responsibility of the presentation order for the fixation times of both Baseline trials and Gaze Direction trials, differences scores were calculated for the fixation duration in each trial separately. Positive scores indicate longer fixations of the attended toy, whereas negative scores demonstrate longer fixations of the unattended toy (see Figure 5). The differences of these scores were analysed by a one-way ANOVA of the changed locations (GD1 to B2, GD2 to B3, GD3 to B4). This analysis revealed no significant main effect, $F(2, 10) = 1.907$, $p = .199$, ruling out an overall influence of the presentation order. Of special interest was the alteration between GD1 and

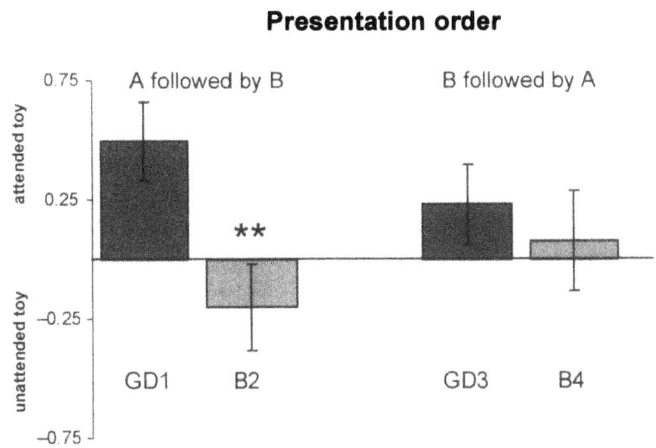

Figure 5. Average difference scores of the fixation duration to the attended and unattended toy, based on AOI, in Baseline trials and Gaze Direction trials in reference to the presentation order. Positive scores indicate longer fixation to the attended toy, negative scores to the unattended toy, respectively. Error bars indicate standard error and ** depict significant differences.

B2 (A followed by B), as well as between GD3 and B4 (B followed by A). Planned contrasts yielded a significant difference of the scores between GD1 ($M = 0.49$, $SE = 0.17$) and B2 ($M = -0.20$, $SE = 0.18$), $t(11) = 3.728$, $p = .003$, indicating a location cueing at the beginning (see Figure 5). Nevertheless, this difference disappeared over trials. Accordingly, the difference scores did not vary anymore during the last changed location between GD3 ($M = 0.23$, $SE = 0.16$) and B4 ($M = 0.08$, $SE = 0.21$), $t(11) = 0.678$, $p = .512$.

DISCUSSION

In order to investigate object processing in a gaze following task, we presented 12-month-old infants with different movies on an eye tracker. The first four movies showed a female model turning and looking to one of two objects; this was followed by two test trials showing only the two objects without the model. Infants did not differentiate between the two objects during the Baseline block. In the Gaze Direction block infants consistently followed the model's gaze to the attended object and fixated the attended longer than the unattended object. No overall difference was found during the Test block; there was, however, a significant difference in the first test trial, here infants fixated the unattended object for a longer duration than the attended object.

First of all, it is important to emphasize that these results complement previous findings that infants by the end of the first year of life follow gaze (Carpenter, Nagell, & Tomasello, 1998; Corkum & Moore, 1995; Johnson et al., 1998; Scaife & Bruner, 1975; von Hofsten et al., 2005), which is an important precondition for the question at hand. In fact, even though the model was presented on a monitor (as opposed to "live"), infants reliably followed the model's gaze to the attended object. This suggests that movies can substitute "live" interactions in order to take advantage of the high resolution provided by current eye-tracking technology.

In addition to demonstrating the basic finding of gaze following, the high spatial-temporal resolution of the eye-tracking system allowed us to obtain additional details about the infants' gaze following behaviour. We were able to differentiate the trials temporally into Baseline, Gaze Direction, and Test blocks, as well as spatially into the three specific areas of interest: face, attended, and unattended objects. This made it possible to show that infants' first fixation of the attended toy differed among the blocks; it was only significantly directed towards the attended toy during the Gaze Direction block. The analysis of the AOIs revealed that the main location of attention was the model's face, where infants spent altogether up to 60% of their looking duration. The first gaze shift from the model's face to a toy during the Gaze Direction block was directed towards the attended toy in 83% of the trials.

Despite the fact that infants readily followed the model's gaze to an object, we cannot find evidence that following another person's gaze direction had a long-term effect on infants' object processing at 12 months of age. The only detectable difference in behaviour towards the attended and the unattended object in the Test block was a brief novelty preference for the previously unattended object. This effect was only evident in the first test trial. We suggest that this result represents a temporarily restricted novelty effect caused by prolonged looking durations to the attended object during the Gaze Direction block.

These results harmonize well with the enhanced object processing documented by Reid and colleagues (2004, 2005). Both studies demonstrate a novelty preference for the previously unattended object. These similarities exist despite differences in the design. In the current study infants were being presented with far more ecologically relevant stimuli that simulated the natural interaction between an infant and an adult.

At the same time the current design allowed us to look at the depth of this enhanced object processing by presenting infants with multiple test trials. We have demonstrated that this novelty effect is brief and only influences infants' behaviour for a single test trial. The current finding suggests that infants do not attribute any strong meaning to the relationship between the model's gaze and the attended object, at least not to such a degree that it has a profound impact on the infant's long-term interaction with the attended object. This suggests that a careful interpretation of the phrase "enhanced object processing" should be applied to future studies of perception of gaze direction. According to our findings, 12-month-old infants follow others' gaze but are unable to represent the relationship between the model's gaze and the attended object, or alternatively are unable to attribute any specificity to the regarded object.

The notion that infants are unable to transfer the perceived relationship between the model and the object across trials receives further support from the infants' performance during the Baseline block. With the exception of the first baseline, infants have previous experience with the model and have perceived her attend to one of the two objects. As such, later parts of the Baseline block could be considered an additional test of infants' object processing. However, as mentioned, no difference in fixation duration was found in this part of each trial. In addition, there was no significant correlation between fixation durations in Gaze Direction and Baseline blocks or between the first gaze shift in the Gaze Direction block and fixation durations during the first test trial. The missing correlation between the looking behaviour during the Gaze direction block and the looking behaviour during the Test block further supports the argument that gaze following does not automatically go hand in hand with object processing.

It is of course possible that by the end of the first test trial infants have fixated the previously unattended object enough to cancel out the novelty effect from the first test trial. Such an alternative interpretation of the current results would produce a similar null-effect in the second test trial. The current design is, however, unable to differentiate between the two.

Interestingly, a study of Itakura (2001) showed that 12-month-old infants looked significantly longer to one of two objects on a screen, if their mother has been previously drawing their attention to it through pointing and vocalizing. In this experiment the infants were sitting on the mother's lap and followed her pointing gesture, not her gaze. The mother's pointing here had a clear impact on the infant's interest towards the attended object.

Consequently, future studies should aim at describing how infants come to attribute a more profound meaning to objects that have been attended by others and to investigate at what age infants attribute sufficient meaning to others' gaze direction to display a stable behavioural change that enhance the acquisition of knowledge about the environment. Related studies (e.g., Itakura, 2001) suggest that additional gestures such as pointing might enhance the processing of the object of interest.

CONCLUSION

The results indicate that infants at the age of 12 months reliably follow others' gaze direction. Nevertheless, there is no implication that retrieving specific information about the objects during a gaze following task is a fundamental property of gaze following at this age. Following a model's gaze does not influence infants' looking behaviour beyond a temporarily restricted response. The study further demonstrates that eye-tracking technology represents a promising paradigm for obtaining detailed information of infants' gaze following. Further investigations are required to observe at what age gaze following results in object processing, which is stable enough to guide long-term interactions with attended objects.

REFERENCES

Bräuer, J., Call, J., & Tomasello, M. (2005). All great apes species follow gaze to distant locations and around barriers. *Journal of Comparative Psychology*, *119*(2), 145–154.

Butterworth, G., & Cochran, E. (1980). Towards a mechanism of joint visual attention in human infancy. *International Journal of Behavioral Development*, *3*, 253–272.

Carpenter, M., Nagell, K., & Tomasello, M. (1998). Social cognition, joint attention, and communicative competence from 9 to 15 months of age. *Monographs of the Society for Research in Child Development*, *63*(4, No. 255), 1–143.

Corkum, V., & Moore, C. (1995). Development of joint visual attention in infants. In C. Moore & P. Dunham (Eds.), *Joint attention. Its origins and role in development* (pp. 61–83). Hillsdale, NJ: Lawrence Erlbaum Associates, Inc.

Corkum, V., & Moore, C. (1998). The origins of joint visual attention in infants. *Developmental Psychology*, *34*(1), 28–38.

D'Entremont, B., Hains, S. M. J., & Muir, D. W. (1997). A demonstration of gaze following in 3- to 6-month-olds. *Infant Behavior and Development*, *20*(4), 569–572.

Flom, R., Deák, G. O., Phill, C. G., & Pick, A. D. (2004). Nine-month-olds' shared visual attention as a function of gesture and object location. *Infant Behavior and Development*, *27*, 181–194.

Gredebäck, G., & von Hofsten, C. (2004). Infants' evolving representations of object motion during occlusion: A longitudinal study of 6- to 12-month-old infants. *Infancy*, *6*(2), 165–184.

Hare, B., Call, J., & Tomasello, M. (1999). Domestic dogs (*Canis familiaris*) use human and conspecific social cues to locate hidden food. *Journal of Comparative Psychology*, *113*, 1–5.

Hood, B. M., Willen, J. D., & Driver, J. (1998). Adult's eyes trigger shifts of visual attention in human infants. *Psychological Science*, *9*(2), 131–134.

Itakura, S. (2001). Attention to repeated events in human infants (*Homo sapiens*): Effects of joint visual attention versus stimulus change. *Animal Cognition*, *4*, 281–284.

Johnson, S., Slaughter, V., & Carey, S. (1998). Whose gaze will infants follow? The elicitation of gaze following in 12-months-olds. *Developmental Science*, *1*(2), 233–238.

Moore, C., & Corkum, V. (1994). Social understanding at the end of the first year of life. *Developmental Review*, *14*, 349–372.

Moore, C., & Corkum, V. (1998). Infants' gaze following based on eye direction. *British Journal of Developmental Psychology*, *16*, 495–503.

Morales, M., Mundy, P., & Rojas, J. (1998). Following the direction of gaze and language development in 6-month-olds. *Infant Behavior and Development*, *21*(2), 373–377.

Morissette, P., Ricard, M., & Gouin Décarie, T. (1995). Joint visual attention and pointing in infancy: A longitudinal study of comprehension. *British Journal of Developmental Psychology*, *13*, 163–175.

Reid, V. M., & Striano, T. (2005). Adult gaze influences infant attention and object processing: Implications for cognitive neuroscience. *European Journal of Neuroscience*, *21*, 1763–1766.

Reid, V. M., Striano, T., Kaufman, J., & Johnson, M. H. (2004). Eye gaze cueing facilitates neural processing of objects in 4-month-old infants. *Neuroreport*, *15*(16), 2553–2555.

Scaife, M., & Bruner, J. S. (1975). The capacity for joint visual attention in the infant. *Nature*, *253*(24), 265–266.

Tomasello, M. (1999). Joint attention and cultural learning. In M. Tomasello (Ed.), *The cultural origins of human cognition* (pp. 56–93). Cambridge, MA: Harvard University Press.

von Hofsten, C., Dahlström, E., & Fredriksson, Y. (2005). 12-months-old infants' perception of attention direction in static video images. *Infancy*, *8*(3), 217–231.

Woodward, A. (2003). Infants' developing understanding of the link between looker and object. *Developmental Science*, *6*(3), 297–311.

EUROPEAN JOURNAL OF DEVELOPMENTAL PSYCHOLOGY
2007, 4 (1), 80–99

Social learning of artefact function in 12- and 15-month-olds

Birgit Elsner and Sabina Pauen
University of Heidelberg, Germany

This study investigates whether infants transfer observed information about the functional use of novel artefacts to their own actions, and whether they generalize this knowledge to perceptually different objects that share the same functional feature. In two experiments, 12- and 15-month-olds performed an imitation task followed by a generalization task. In the imitation task, the same target act was demonstrated with two simple monochrome objects fitted with a specific part, producing a sound effect with one object, but no salient effects with the other object. Infants in both age groups increased their actions on the objects after the demonstration, but only the 15-month-olds preferred to use the "effective" object. This suggests that younger infants learned knowledge about the general function of the objects, whereas older infants learned knowledge about the objects' specific function. In the following generalization task, infants watched no demonstration, but were presented with complex multicoloured objects fitted with the same functional part as the demonstration objects. Both age groups generalized the acquired functional knowledge to the novel objects. Yet, the specificity of the functional information acquired in social learning situations changed between 12 and 15 months of age, which may not only affect the learning of tool use, but also the categorization of artefacts.

Function, that is, what objects do or what can be done with them, appears to be the most prominent feature of man-made artefacts (Nelson, 1973). Consequently, learning about object function is thought to be important for several domains of cognitive development, like object categorization (e.g., Mandler, 2003; Nelson & Ware, 2002) or word learning (Kemler Nelson, 1995). To detect an object's function, one typically has to watch the object

---

Correspondence should be addressed to Birgit Elsner, Department of Psychology, University of Heidelberg, Hauptstrasse 47–51, D-69117 Heidelberg, Germany.
E-mail: elsner@psychologie.uni-heidelberg.de

Much appreciation is due to the infants and parents who participated in this research. Special thanks to Wencke Brusniak for her assistance in data collection and coding. We also thank Christiane Fauth-Scheurich, Jasmin Gruner, Nancy Günther, Stefanie Höhl, and Silja Kennecke for making the appointments, running the experiments and scoring the video tapes.

DOI: 10.1080/17405620601051220

while it moves or while it is used by another person (Madole & Oakes, 1999). When an infant observes another person's use of an object, s/he may acquire two kinds of functional knowledge: First, knowledge about form–function relations, for example, about the relation between function and either the object's shape or the presence of certain parts (e.g., objects used for cutting have a blade). This knowledge may then be generalized to other artefacts that have a similar shape or similar parts, eventually resulting in the formation of an object category (e.g., tools for cutting). Second, knowledge about the effective use of an object (e.g., a knife needs to be moved back and forth in order to cut). In this case, the model's actions have to be transferred to own behaviour (Tomasello, 1999). In developmental psychology, infants' ability to use observed functional information for object categorization and to reproduce other persons' actions on objects are investigated in separate lines of research.

Categorization of artefacts is mainly studied in paradigms that assess infants' attention to several objects. These studies indicate developmental changes in the ability to detect form–function relations during the first two years of life. Ten-month-old infants, who have been familiarized with the same action performed on different objects, increase their attention when a familiar object is combined with a novel action (Horst, Oakes, & Madole, 2005). By 14 to 18 months, infants who have been familiarized with two objects, each of which was combined with a certain action, dishabituate to novel combinations of the familiar objects and actions (Madole & Cohen, 1995; Madole, Oakes, & Cohen, 1993). Infants aged 14 and 18 months can also attend to relations between function and the presence of certain object parts (Booth & Waxman, 2002). Infants had been familiarized with different objects that shared the same functional part and served the same purpose (e.g., objects with a loop were hung on a hook). When infants were asked to hand the experimenter the one of two novel objects that was most similar to the familiarization objects, they preferentially chose an object that featured the familiar functional part. Hence, infants can relate an object's shape or the presence of certain object parts to its function, and they generalize the observed function to novel objects that share the same functional shape or parts.

To investigate learning about the functional relevance of object parts in younger infants, Träuble and Pauen (in press) presented 11- to 12-month-olds with novel objects that were coloured and had several side parts, one of which was T-shaped (see Figure 1). In one condition, infants were familiarized with different objects that featured the T-part in the same orientation, and got an object with the T-part in another orientation at test. Without prior demonstration, infants did not dishabituate to the test object, and thus did not categorize the objects according to T-part orientation. However, after having watched the experimenter performing actions and producing effects with simple white objects that featured differently oriented T-parts, infants

Figure 1. Test objects used in Experiment 1 and Experiment 2. Upper left: effect box; lower left: monochrome simple objects of the imitation task; right: coloured multi-part objects of the generalization task. Half of the generalization objects were in reddish colours and had rounded side parts, the other half were in bluish colours and had angular side parts.

classified the coloured multi-part objects according to T-part orientation. If the model's actions produced no effects, however, infants again did not use this feature for categorization. Thus, observing the demonstration of the T-part's effectiveness enabled 11- to 12-month-old infants to use a non-salient perceptual property for detecting similarities between novel artefacts. This required that infants not only encoded the T-parts' function but also generalized this information to perceptually dissimilar objects.

Thus far, studies on object categorization have neglected whether infants would transfer the observed functional information to their own actions, that is, whether they would use novel artefacts in the modelled way. Infants' ability to reproduce other persons' actions is investigated in imitation studies. These studies assess infants' behaviour on certain test objects after the infants have observed a model performing a certain target action on these objects. However, imitation studies typically focus on infants' learning of the modelled target acts (see Meltzoff, 2002, or Uzgiris, 1999, for reviews), and only few of them address what infants learn about the objects involved. One of these studies (Barnat, Klein, & Meltzoff, 1996) revealed that 14-month-olds generalized observed target acts to novel test objects that varied from the original demonstration objects in both colour and size. Although infants' performance was best with the original objects, the novel-object group still executed more target acts than a control group who had not seen any demonstration. In a study by Hayne, MacDonald, and Barr (1997), 12-month-olds generalized modelled target acts to a novel object that varied in colour from the original object, but not to objects that varied in shape, or in both colour and shape. If infants generalize target acts to novel artefacts that share functional attributes with the demonstration objects, this may be taken as an active measure of object categorization.

Whereas the function of objects is that they do certain things or allow certain things to be done with them, the function of actions is to attain certain goals or produce certain effects (Elsner & Hommel, 2001). Generally, the presence of salient action effects facilitates infants' reproduction of observed actions (e.g., Bellagamba & Tomasello, 1999; Huang, Heyes, & Charman, 2002). Hauf, Elsner, and Aschersleben (2004) reported that of two observed actions, 12- and 18-month-olds preferentially imitated the one that was followed by a salient action effect. Several imitation studies provide evidence that the ability to learn relations between observed actions and their effects emerges between 9 and 12 months of age (Carpenter, Nagell, & Tomasello, 1998; Provasi, Dubon, & Bloch, 2001). During the second year of life, the acquired action–effect relations become increasingly specific, enabling the infant to detect novel combinations between familiar actions and familiar effects (Elsner & Aschersleben, 2003). Hence, infants are able to relate the occurrence of an effect to a certain action, and they prefer an observed action that led to a salient effect for their own behaviour.

The main goal of the present study was to combine these two lines of research and investigate infants' learning about object function in an imitation paradigm. In particular, we conducted an imitation task and a generalization task to see whether 12- and 15-month-olds would transfer observed information about the function of novel artefacts to their own actions, and whether they would generalize the eventually acquired functional knowledge to perceptually dissimilar objects that share the same functional part. To be able to compare infants' performance in the present tasks and in a categorization task, we used the same objects as Träuble and Pauen (in press). The imitation task was conducted with monochrome simple objects and the generalization task with coloured multi-part objects (see Figure 1).

In the imitation task, the experimenter demonstrated the same target act with two simple objects. Each object consisted of a white cube with a black T-shaped side part, with either the vertical or the horizontal T-bar pointing away from the cube. The T-part of each object was lowered to a hole of an effect box. The pin-like T-part of the one object fitted into the hole, and the action produced a sound effect (i.e., effective object). The anchor-like T-part of the other object did not fit into the hole, and the action did not lead to any salient effect (i.e., ineffective object). Based on the findings by Hauf et al. (2004), we expected that infants who learned the specific relations between the orientation of the T-part and the presence of the effect would prefer the effective object for their own actions. In contrast, infants who encoded the general action performed with both objects (i.e., lowering the T-part towards the hole) should use both objects about equally often.

The generalization task was conducted after the imitation task. In this task, we presented infants with the effect box and two coloured multi-part objects: one with an effective, and the other with an ineffective T-part. Although the function of the coloured objects was never demonstrated, infants who generalized their eventually acquired functional knowledge should lower the T-part of the coloured multi-part objects to the box. Again, infants who generalized specific form – function relations should prefer the coloured object with the effective T-part, whereas infants who generalized the objects' general function should use both coloured objects about equally often.

EXPERIMENT 1

The goal of Experiment 1 was to assess social learning and generalization of object function in 12-month-olds. Infants of this age learn the function of objects in visual paradigms (Horst et al., 2005), they learn action – effect relations by observation (Elsner & Aschersleben, 2003), and they are able to use observed functional information about the T-part for the categorization of novel artefacts (Träuble & Pauen, in press).

Method

Participants

The final sample consisted of 24 healthy full-term infants with a mean age of 12 months and 13 days (range: 12;01 to 12;30, 11 girls, 13 boys). An additional 11 infants were tested but excluded from the analyses because of fussiness ($n = 6$) or parental interference ($n = 5$). Infants' names were obtained from birth records, and their families were contacted by letter and phone calls. Parents received a certificate with their child's photo for participating.

Materials

The objects in this study were the same as those used by Träuble and Pauen (in press). The objects were specially constructed, so the infants could not have seen them before.

In the imitation task, the objects were a grey effect box (16 × 13 × 5 cm) and two white cubes (side length: 3.5 cm), each of which had a black T-shaped appendix (length: 3 cm). The vertical T-bar protruded from one cube, the horizontal T-bar from the other (see Figure 1). On the top of the effect box, there was a small red block with a round hole. The stick-like T-part could be inserted into the hole, which activated a buzzer inside the box. The anchor-like T-part did not fit into the hole. The cube with the stick-like T-part is termed "effective object", the cube with the anchor-like T-part "ineffective object".

In the generalization task, the same grey box and six additional objects were used (see Figure 1). These objects were coloured cubes (side length: 3.5 cm) with four different side parts (length: 3 cm). Three of the objects were in reddish colours and had rounded side parts, and three were in bluish colours and had angular side parts. One of the side parts was a black T-shaped appendage, identical to that of the white objects described above. Not one of the other side parts could be inserted into the hole, so these parts were irrelevant to the task. The vertical T-bar protruded from three of the objects (i.e., effective objects), whereas the horizontal T-bar protruded from the other three (i.e., ineffective objects).

Design and procedure

Infants were seated in a high chair with an attached tray. The caregiver sat to the infant's right, and the experimenter sat opposite. In a short warm-up period, the experimenter handed the infant some toys. The experiment consisted of eight 20 s trials in which the objects were put into the infant's reach for exploration, and four demonstration phases in which the experimenter performed the target act with the effective and the ineffective simple object. The experiment lasted about 5 minutes and was videotaped for later coding. Across trials and infants, we counterbalanced whether the effective or ineffective object was placed to the left or the right of the box, and whether the demonstration started with the effective or ineffective object.

The first two trials were baseline trials to assess infants' spontaneous behaviour on the objects used in the imitation or the generalization task, respectively. In trial 1, infants explored the box and the two monochrome objects for 20 s. Then, all objects were removed. In trial 2, infants explored the box, one reddish-round object with an effective T-part, and one bluish-angular object with an ineffective T-part.

Trials 3 to 6 were the imitation trials. Prior to each trial, the experimenter put the box on the tray, out of the infant's reach. After having directed the child's attention to the objects, the experimenter demonstrated the target act with one of the objects, while the other object was put left or right of the box. The experimenter did not speak during demonstration. The target act was to lower the T-part to the box, touching the hole with the far end. The effective T-part was inserted into the hole, thereby producing a sound effect. The ineffective T-part just touched the hole, not producing any salient effect.

The target act was demonstrated with each object three times in succession prior to trial 3, and once prior to trials 4 to 6. After each demonstration phase, the box and the two objects were put into the infant's reach for a 20s exploration. The imitation trials were to assess whether infants would apply observed information about the general and/or the specific function of the T-parts to their own actions. We conducted four imitation trials to be able to track the course of social learning across trials, and to give the infants the opportunity to gather enough information.

Trials 7 and 8 served as generalization trials. There was no demonstration prior to these trials, but the objects were immediately put into the infant's reach for a 20s exploration. In both trials, the box was presented together with two reddish-round or bluish-angular objects, one fitted with an effective, and the other with an ineffective T-part. The generalization trials were to assess whether infants would transfer the eventually acquired functional knowledge from the imitation task to perceptually dissimilar objects fitted with the same T-part.

Coding

Infants' behaviour during the eight 20 s trials was scored by two independent coders according to two categories: (1) performance of target acts and (2) manipulation time.

(1) Coders recorded how often the infant lowered the effective or ineffective T-part to the hole. Here, attempts to insert the T-part into the hole, or the use of an irrelevant side part of the coloured objects, were also coded as target acts.

(2) Because inserting the T-part into the hole may have been difficult for the younger infants, coders additionally recorded the duration of episodes in which the infant touched the box with the effective or ineffective object. Infants who noticed the specific function should prefer the effective object for these behaviours as well. Because we were interested in active exploratory behaviours, this category was only coded when infants looked at their actions.

Interrater reliability was high, ranging from $r = .92$ to $r = .99$ (average $r = .96$). The analyses were based on the mean scores of both coders on any given trial. An alpha level of .05 was used for all statistical tests, one-tailed for planned comparisons.

Results

Imitation task

Target acts. Table 1 displays the number of infants who lowered the T-part of the effective or the ineffective object to the hole as a function of

TABLE 1
Numbers of infants who performed the target act in the trials of the two tasks

	Imitation task					*Generalization task*		
Object used	*Baseline 1*	*Imit. 1*	*Imit. 2*	*Imit. 3*	*Imit. 4*	*Baseline 2*	*Gen. 1*	*Gen. 2*
Experiment 1: 12-month-olds								
Eff. only	1	2	4	5	2	1	2	3
Ineff. only	0	2	1	2	3	0	2	3
Both objects	0	1	0	0	0	0	0	0
No target acts	23	19	19	17	19	23	20	18
Experiment 2: 15-month-olds								
Eff. only	0	7	8	9	11	2	8	6
Ineff. only	1	6	5	6	1	1	6	6
Both objects	0	3	4	4	6	0	3	2
No target acts	23	8	7	5	6	21	7	10

Note: $n = 24$ for each experiment. It was coded whether the infant performed the target act during each 20 s trial and, if so, which object was used. Eff. only = only the effective object was used; Ineff. only = only the ineffective object was used; No target acts = infants did not perform any target acts.

trial (baseline 1, imitation trials 1 to 4). The number of infants who did so increased significantly from the baseline to the first imitation trial, $\chi^2(1, n = 48) = 3.1$, $p < .05$, but stayed about the same across the further imitation trials. Thus, some infants learned the target act by observing the first demonstration, but they did not benefit from the repeated demonstrations. Most infants performed the target act with only one of the objects, but there was no preference for the effective object.

The average number of target acts (including attempts) performed by the infants as a function of trial (baseline 1, imitation trials 1 to 4) and object (effective vs ineffective) is shown in Figure 2. A 5 × 2 analysis of variance (ANOVA) with trial and object as within-subject variables yielded only a significant main effect of trial, $F(4, 92) = 2.8$, $p < .05$. Planned comparisons over adjacent trials revealed that the number of target acts increased significantly from the baseline to the first imitation trial, $t(23) = -2.5$, $p < .02$, and from the second to the third imitation trial, $t(23) = -2.2$, $p < .03$, but did not differ across the further trials (all $ps > .23$). Thus, some of the 12-month-olds performed more target acts after having seen repeated demonstrations. But again, there was no preference for one of the objects.

Manipulation times. Figure 3 displays the cumulated times in which the infants touched the box with the effective or ineffective object as a function

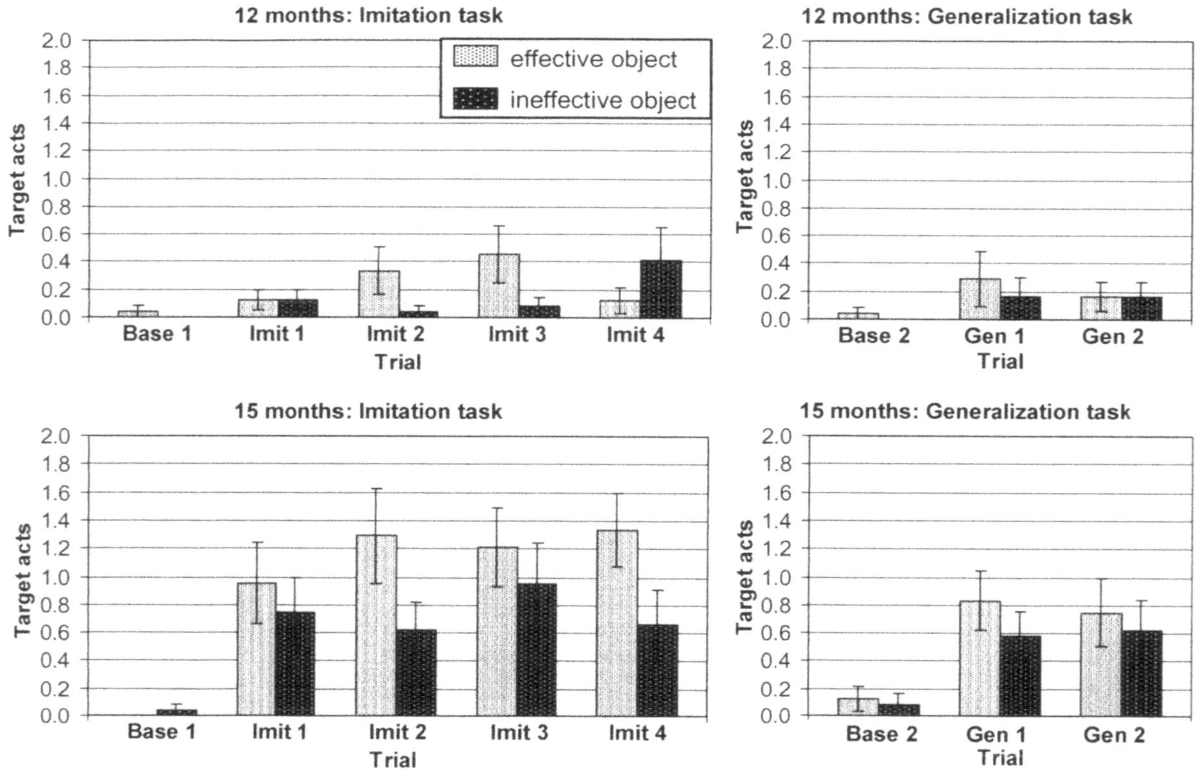

Figure 2. Mean number of target acts (+*SE*) performed with the effective or ineffective object in each trial of the two tasks in Experiment 1 (12-month-olds) and Experiment 2 (15-month-olds).

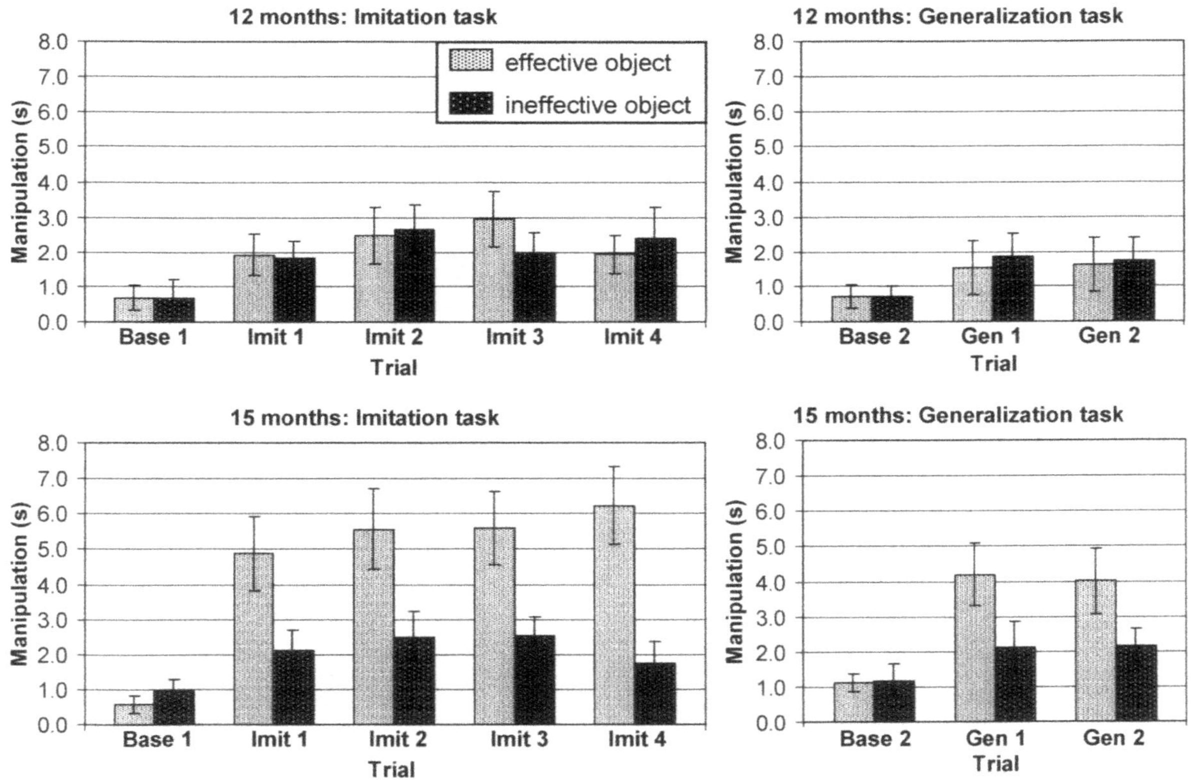

Figure 3. Mean manipulation times (+*SE*) with the effective or ineffective object in each trial of the two tasks in Experiment 1 (12-month-olds) and Experiment 2 (15-month-olds).

of trial. A 5 (trial) × 2 (object) ANOVA yielded only a significant main effect of trial, $F(4, 92) = 4.8$, $p < .002$. The manipulation times increased significantly from the baseline to the first imitation trial, $t(23) = -2.5$, $p < .02$, but did not differ across the further trials (all $ps > .08$). The first demonstration thus stimulated the infants to touch the box with the objects, and they did not benefit from the further demonstrations. In neither trial did the infants prefer one of the objects.

Generalization task

Target acts. Table 1 displays the number of infants who performed (or tried to perform) the target act with a side part of the effective or ineffective coloured object as a function of trial (baseline 2, generalization trials 1 and 2). The number of infants who did so was low and did not differ significantly between the trials (all $ps > .05$). Hence, only a few of the infants tried to insert the T-part, or one of the other side parts, of the coloured objects into the hole.

The average number of target acts (including attempts) as a function of trial and object is shown in Figure 2. A 3 (trial) × 2 (object) ANOVA yielded no significant main effects or interactions (all $ps > .12$). The average number of target acts performed with the coloured objects was too small to generate any significant results.

Manipulation times. Figure 3 displays the cumulated manipulation times for the effective or ineffective coloured object as a function of trial. A 3 (trial) × 2 (object) ANOVA yielded only a significant main effect of trial, $F(2, 46) = 3.5$, $p < .05$. Infants' manipulation times increased significantly from the baseline to the first generalization trial, $t(23) = -2.0$, $p < .03$, but did not differ between the two generalization trials ($p = .46$). Thus, 12-month-olds generalized touching the box to the coloured objects, but they did not prefer one of the objects.

Discussion

Experiment 1 provided evidence that 12-month-old infants learned the general function of the novel artefacts by observation and applied this information in their own actions. Infants seem to have encoded that the objects are to be brought in contact with the box. None of the dependent variables revealed a preference for either the effective or the ineffective object, indicating that the infants did not acquire the specific function of the T-part. In the imitation task, both the number of performed target acts and the times in which infants touched the box with either simple object increased from the baseline to the first imitation trial. It has to be noted, however, that the absolute number of infants performing the target act was rather small. The infants did not benefit from additional demonstrations, because their performance changed only negligibly in further imitation trials.

The dependent variables of the generalization task allow different inferences about 12-month-olds' ability to generalize the acquired functional knowledge to perceptually dissimilar objects sharing the same functional part: The manipulation times indicate generalization of the acquired general function. Although infants had never observed the experimenter bringing the coloured objects in contact with the box, their manipulation times increased from the baseline to the first generalization trial. However, infants only occasionally performed the target act with the coloured objects. We will come back to the possible reasons for this dissociation in the generalization measures in the general discussion.

EXPERIMENT 2

In Experiment 2, we investigated social learning and generalization of object function in 15-month-old infants. In object categorization tasks, infants this age encode form–function relations (Booth & Waxman, 2002; Madole & Cohen, 1995), and in imitation tasks, they learn specific relations between actions and effects (Elsner & Aschersleben, 2003). These capabilities could help 15-month-olds to detect the specific function of the T-part when observing the model's actions.

Method

Participants

The final sample consisted of 24 healthy, full-term, infants with a mean age of 15 months and 15 days (range: 15;02 to 15;25, 12 girls, 12 boys). An additional 9 infants were tested but were excluded from the analyses because of fussiness ($n = 2$) or procedural errors ($n = 7$). None of the infants had participated in Experiment 1.

Materials, design and procedure

The test environment, material, design, and procedure were identical to those of Experiment 1.

Scoring

The scoring was identical to that of Experiment 1. Interrater reliability was high, ranging from $r = .97$ to $r = .99$ (average $r = .98$).

Results

Imitation task

Target acts. Table 1 displays the number of infants who performed the target act with the effective or ineffective monochrome object as a function of trial (baseline 1, imitation trials 1 to 4). The number of infants increased significantly from the baseline to the first imitation trial, $\chi^2(1, n=48)=20.5$, $p<.001$, and stayed about the same across the further imitation trials. Thus, the 15-month-olds imitated the target act after the first demonstration, but they did not benefit from repeated demonstrations.

The average number of performed target acts (including attempts) as a function of trial and object is shown in Figure 2. A 5 (trial) × 2 (object) ANOVA yielded significant main effects of trial, $F(4, 92)=14.4$, $p<.001$, and of object, $F(1, 23)=5.9$, $p<.03$, but no significant interaction ($p=.66$). The number of target acts increased significantly from the baseline to the first imitation trial, $t(23)=-4.8$, $p<.001$, and stayed about the same across the further trials (all *ps* > .18). Infants performed more target acts with the effective ($M=4.8$, $SD=3.5$) than with the ineffective object ($M=3.0$, $SD=2.9$). Hence, the 15-month-olds learned to perform the target act by observation, and they preferred the effective object for their own actions. This suggests that they had encoded the specific function of the T-part.

Manipulation times. Figure 3 displays the manipulation times for the effective and the ineffective object as a function of trial. A 5 (trial) × 2 (object) ANOVA yielded significant main effects of trial $F(4, 92)=18.4$, $p<.001$, and of object, $F(1, 23)=13.8$, $p<.005$, but no significant interaction ($p=.11$). The main effect of trial was due to an increase in the manipulation times from the baseline to the first imitation trial, $t(23)=-6.5$, $p<.001$. Manipulation times stayed about the same across the further trials (all *ps* > .11). The main effect of object was due to longer manipulation times for the effective ($M=22.9$ s, $SD=15.2$) than for the ineffective object ($M=9.8$ s, $SD=6.9$). The infants thus not only preferred to perform the target acts, but also to touch the box, with the effective object.

Generalization task

Target acts. The number of infants performing the target act with the effective or ineffective coloured object increased significantly from the baseline to the first generalization trial, $\chi^2(1, n=48)=16.8$, $p<.001$, but did not differ between the two generalization trials (see Table 1). The infants showed no preference for one of the coloured objects.

This was also confirmed by the average number of target acts (see Figure 2). A 3 (trial) × 2 (object) ANOVA yielded only a significant main effect of trial, $F(2, 46) = 12.3$, $p < .001$. The number of target acts increased significantly from the baseline to the first generalization trial, $t(23) = -4.6$, $p < .001$, and did not differ between the two generalization trials ($p = .88$). Thus, the 15-month-olds generalized the knowledge that the objects' side parts could be lowered to the hole. However, infants performed about the same number of target acts with the effective or the ineffective coloured object.

Manipulation times. Figure 3 displays the manipulation times for the effective and ineffective coloured object as a function of trial. A 3 (trial) × 2 (object) ANOVA yielded significant main effects of trial, $F(2, 46) = 11.9$, $p < .001$, and of object, $F(1, 23) = 4.3$, $p = .05$, but no significant interaction ($p = .36$). The manipulation times increased significantly from the baseline to the first generalization trial, $t(23) = -4.1$, $p < .001$, but did not differ between the two generalization trials ($p = .44$). The manipulation times for the effective object ($M = 9.3$, $SD = 7.0$) were higher than for the ineffective object ($M = 5.4$, $SD = 5.2$). Thus, the 15-month-old infants preferred to touch the box with the effective coloured multi-part object, which indicates that they generalized the specific function of the simple objects.

Discussion

Experiment 2 revealed that 15-month-old infants learned the specific function of the simple objects by observation and applied this knowledge to their own actions. In the imitation task, infants performed more target acts with the effective object, and they also preferred to touch the box with the effective object. The first demonstration had the highest impact on infants' behaviour; infants did not benefit from the further demonstrations. The 15-month-olds also generalized the acquired functional knowledge to the coloured multi-part objects. Infants performed more target acts, and they also touched the box more often, with the coloured objects in the first generalization trial than during baseline, albeit they had never observed the experimenter doing this. Yet, like in Experiment 1, the generalization measures led to different implications about 15-month-olds' generalization ability: Infants preferred the effective object only for touching the box, not for their performance of target acts. Hence, only the manipulation times revealed generalization of the acquired specific function, whereas the performance of target actions indicated generalization of the general function.

GENERAL DISCUSSION

The experiments reported here provide evidence that 12- and 15-month-old infants learn the function of novel artefacts when they observe another person's actions with these objects, and that they transfer the observed functional information to their own actions quite rapidly. However, infants in the two age groups differed according to the specificity of the acquired functional knowledge: Fifteen-month-olds preferred the effective object when performing the target act or touching the box, that is, they chose the object that had produced a salient action effect during demonstration. This requires that they had encoded the specific function of the T-part when observing the model's actions and applied this information to their own actions. Contrary to this, 12-month-olds showed no preference for the effective object, neither when performing the target act, which they did only infrequently, nor when touching the box the objects. The younger infants probably did not learn the relations between the orientation of the T-part and the presence of the sound, but encoded the objects' general function. Hence, the present results suggest important progress with respect to infants' learning about artefact function in social situations between 12 and 15 months of age.

The second important finding was that infants of both age groups generalized the acquired functional knowledge to perceptually dissimilar objects sharing the same functional part. The pattern of findings for the generalization trials resembles that for the imitation task in both age groups: Twelve-month-olds brought both coloured multi-part objects in contact with the box, albeit they had never observed the model doing so, thus generalizing the objects' general function. Yet, they did not prefer the object with the effective T-part, and they did not perform more target acts than during baseline. Fifteen-month-olds preferred to touch the box with the effective coloured object, thus generalizing the objects' specific function. They also performed more target acts in the generalization trials than during baseline, but they did not prefer the effective object for doing so. These results imply that generalization of functional knowledge to perceptually different objects does not change much between 12 and 15 months of age, and we will come back to this below. What seems to change is the specificity of the acquired functional information. This raises questions as to why 12-month-olds did not prefer the effective object and did not perform many target acts with the presented material.

It seems quite improbable that the perceptual or motor demands of the task can account for our findings: There is evidence that 12-month-olds are well able to attend to the shape and the function of objects in categorization tasks (e.g., Horst et al., 2005; Madole et al., 1993). Furthermore, in the study by Träuble and Pauen (in press), who used the same objects, 11- to 12-month-olds discriminated the orientation of the T-part after having seen a demonstration of that part's function. To reduce the motor demands of the task, we included attempts to perform the target acts in our scoring. Infants were only required to touch the hole with the far end of the T-part to be judged as performing the target act. Moreover, the scoring of manipulation times just required that the box was touched with the objects. At 12 months, infants manipulate objects quite effectively (e.g., McCarty, Clifton, & Collard, 2001), and even if the younger infants had difficulty in performing the target act, they could have shown their preference for the effective object in the manipulation times. Given the fact that neither perceptual nor motor problems can account for the lack of specific-function learning in 12-month-olds, it might be worthwhile to consider certain aspects of the social situation in which learning took place.

Social learning of artefact function

In the present study, we demonstrated the same target act with both objects (i.e., lowering the T-part towards a hole in the effect box), producing the sound only with the effective, but not with the ineffective object. We reasoned that it would be quite easy for the infants to detect the specific function of the objects when they had to monitor only one action and one effect, the latter being either present or absent. In a similar paradigm where one, but not another action with the same object produced an effect, 12-month-olds preferentially performed the effective movement (Hauf et al., 2004). These two paradigms are similar in terms of complexity, but different in terms of what infants had to attend to: In Hauf et al.'s study, infants had to relate the occurrence of the effect to a specific action, whereas in our study, infants had to relate this to a specific object. In imitation studies, 12-month-olds learn relations between actions and effects (e.g., Carpenter et al., 1998; Elsner & Aschersleben, 2003; Provasi et al., 2001), and this capability may have helped them to discriminate the actions in Hauf et al.'s study. However, in the present study, the fact that the experimenter performed the same action with each object may have drawn the younger infants' attention away from the objects, leading them to treat the T-parts as similar.

This would also explain why 12-month-olds learned to attend to the T-part in the study by Träuble and Pauen (in press), but not in the present study. Träuble and Pauen used a different box and presented two actions and effects: The stick-like T-part of the one object was inserted into a hole to produce a sound (just like in the present study), and the anchor-like T-part of the other object was used to pull two hooks to produce a visual effect. Hence, the experimenter performed different actions, and produced diverging effects, with the two objects. This may have helped the infants to attend to the perceptual differences of the T-parts. It should be noted, however, that in Träuble and Pauen's study, demonstrating the same actions without producing any effects did not lead to categorization according to T-part orientation. This suggests that watching different actions with each object was not sufficient, but that the specific form–function information was only encoded when the actions led to salient effects. This corresponds to findings that actions that lead to salient effects are preferentially replicated in imitation studies (e.g., Bellagamba & Tomasello, 1999; Hauf et al., 2004; Huang et al., 2002). In the present study, the occurrence of the effect was not related to a specific action, but to a specific object, and younger infants seemingly failed to encode this relation.

It may be speculated that 12-month-olds' attentive capacities are not yet sufficient to co-ordinate the perceptual features of the three objects involved in the present demonstration, the motor features of the target act, and the relation between the orientation of the T-part and the presence or absence of the sound effect. Other imitation studies also provide evidence that younger infants sometimes do not encode all aspects of target-action demonstrations. For instance, Elsner and Aschersleben (2003) reported that 12-month-olds performed more target acts after having observed the demonstration, but did not detect whether their own actions produced the same effects as the model's actions. This was taken as evidence that infants had learned general relations between the observed movements and effects (i.e., something interesting happened when performing the target acts), but they had not learned the specific relations between each movement and its effect.

Likewise, in the present study, the 12-month-olds seem to have encoded the general, but not the specific, function of the objects during demonstration. Thus, it may be speculated that in social learning situations, 12-month-olds mainly focus on the activity demonstrated by the experimenter, and that the presence of action effects helps them to encode these actions. When the observed actions differentiate between the objects involved, infants discriminate the objects' specific functional relevance (Träuble & Pauen, in press). However, when the observed actions highlight the similarity of the objects, and only the effects suggest dissimilarity, 12-month-olds fail to encode the specific relation between the objects' form and their function—at least when the perceptual differences between the objects are quite subtle, as was the case in the present study.

The 15-month-old infants in the present study appear to extract more specific information from the demonstration and transfer this knowledge to their own actions. To be able to prefer the effective object, these infants must not only have discriminated the orientation of the T-parts, but also have related the occurrence of the sound to one specific T-part. Their developed abilities to attend to relations between the objects' shape or parts and its function (Booth & Waxman, 2002; Madole et al., 1993; Madole & Cohen, 1995) and to learn specific associations between actions and effects (Elsner & Aschersleben, 2003) may have been helpful for this. Thus, the major lesson to be learned from the reported set of findings is that 12-month-olds' ability to co-ordinate information about objects, actions, and effects is still limited in social learning situations, but seems to show rapid progress in the following three months, leading to substantially improved performance at 15 months of age.

Generalization of functional knowledge

In both age groups, infants generalized the functional knowledge they had acquired with the monochrome simple objects to the coloured multi-part objects. The 12-month-olds generalized the objects' general function, the 15-months-olds the specific function. This corresponds to findings that 14-month-olds are able to transfer target actions to objects that differ in size and colour (Barnat et al., 1996). However, Hayne et al. (1997) reported that 12-month-olds failed to perform the target actions when the test object varied in form, or in form and colour, from the original object. The present study differed from the latter study in that infants practised the target acts with the simple objects before handling the coloured objects. Thus, when using the coloured multi-part objects, they relied not only on knowledge acquired by observation, but also on knowledge acquired by own actions. For 18-month-old infants, Hayne, Barr, and Herbert (2003) reported that practising the target acts facilitated generalization. The present findings suggest that this may also be the case for younger infants.

Infants' generalization of object function was mainly apparent in the manipulation times. Most likely, the presence of the irrelevant side parts affected infants' target-act performance in the generalization trials. The discrimination of the effective and the ineffective object was probably more difficult in the generalization task than in the imitation task, because both objects had irrelevant side parts. Moreover, because the coloured multi-part objects were more attractive than the simple objects, infants' attention may have been drawn to the objects, thus dampening target-act performance. This may be the reason why 12-month-olds did not generalize the target act to the coloured objects.

The 15-month-olds had encoded the specific function of the simple objects; so they seem to have learned that the effective T-part was needed to produce the sound effect. This understanding of the form – function relation may have had opposite effects on generalization: On the one hand, infants may have focused on the orientation of the T-part, which should facilitate the identification of the effective coloured object. On the other hand, infants may have been distracted by the irrelevant side parts, because they did not realize that these parts did not fit into the hole. This should impede the discrimination of the coloured objects. The 15-month-olds preferred the effective coloured object for touching the box, indicating that they were able to discriminate between the objects. However, they did not prefer the effective object for performing the target act, indicating that they had been distracted by the irrelevant side parts. It may be speculated that for target-act performance, the learner has to extract more of the demonstrated information than for manipulation, like the exact movement path or the relation between certain object parts and the occurrence of the sound effect. Generalization of functional knowledge to perceptually different objects requires additional mental effort, and this could explain why infants' generalization was more apparent in the manipulation times.

Learning about artefact functions in natural social settings is quite a demanding task. It typically requires the infant to attend to specific features of a given object, to understand the relations between the object's shape or parts and its function, to closely monitor the movements of another person performed on the artefact, and also to encode the specific effects produced by the observed actions. Furthermore, infants need to organize their own imitative behaviour, and they need to transfer knowledge from one situation or one object to another to build up generalized knowledge about the functional relevance of different sets of artefacts. Keeping the complexity of these different task demands in mind, it does not come as a surprise that the social learning of artefact function shows considerable progress throughout the second year of life.

REFERENCES

Barnat, S. B., Klein, P. J., & Meltzoff, A. N. (1996). Deferred imitation across changes in context and object: Memory and generalization in 14-month-old infants. *Infant Behavior & Development*, *19*, 241–251.

Bellagamba, F., & Tomasello, M. (1999). Re-enacting intended acts: Comparing 12- and 18-month olds. *Infant Behavior & Development*, *22*, 277–282.

Booth, A. E., & Waxman, S. (2002). Object names and object functions serve as cues to categorization for infants. *Developmental Psychology*, *38*, 948–957.

Carpenter, M., Nagell, K., & Tomasello, M. (1998). Social cognition, joint attention, and communicative competence from 9 to 15 months of age. *Monographs of the Society for Research in Child Development*, *63*, 1–176.

Elsner, B., & Aschersleben, G. (2003). Do I get what you get? Learning about the effects of self-performed and observed action in infancy. *Consciousness & Cognition*, *12*, 732–751.

Elsner, B., & Hommel, B. (2001). Effect anticipation and action control. *Journal of Experimental Psychology: Human Perception and Performance*, *27*, 229–240.

Hauf, P., Elsner, B., & Aschersleben, G. (2004). The role of action-generated effects in infant imitation. *Psychological Research*, *68*, 115–125.

Hayne, H., Barr, R., & Herbert, J. (2003). The effect of prior practice on memory reactivation and generalization. *Child Development*, *74*, 1615–1627.

Hayne, H., MacDonald, S., & Barr, R. (1997). Developmental changes in the specificity of memory over the second year of life. *Infant Behavior & Development*, *20*, 233–245.

Horst, J. S., Oakes, L. M., & Madole, K. L. (2005). What does it look like and what can it do? Category structure influences how infants categorize. *Child Development*, *76*, 614–631.

Huang, C.-T., Heyes, C., & Charman, T. (2002). Infants' behavioral reenactment of "failed attempts": Exploring the roles of emulation learning, stimulus enhancement, and understanding of intentions. *Developmental Psychology*, *38*, 840–855.

Kemler Nelson, D. G. (1995). Principle-based inferences in young children's categorization. Revisiting the impact of function on the naming of artefacts. *Cognitive Development*, *10*, 347–380.

Madole, K. L., & Cohen, L. B. (1995). The role of object parts in infants' attention to form–function correlations. *Developmental Psychology*, *31*, 637–648.

Madole, K. L., & Oakes, L. M. (1999). Making sense of infant categorization: Stable processes and changing representations. *Developmental Review*, *19*, 263–296.

Madole, K. L., Oakes, L. M., & Cohen, L. B. (1993). Developmental changes in infants' attention to function and form–function correlations. *Cognitive Development*, *8*, 189–209.

Mandler, J. M. (2003). Conceptual categorization. In D. H. Rakison & L. M. Oakes (Eds.), *Early category and concept development: Making sense of the blooming, buzzing confusion* (pp. 103–131). New York: Oxford University Press.

McCarty, M. E., Clifton, R. K., & Collard, R. R. (2001). The beginnings of tool use by infants and toddlers. *Infancy*, *2*, 233–256.

Meltzoff, A. N. (2002). Elements of a developmental theory of imitation. In A. N. Meltzoff & W. Prinz (Eds.), *The imitative mind* (pp. 19–41). Cambridge, UK: Cambridge University Press.

Nelson, K. (1973). Some evidence for the cognitive primacy of categorization and its functional bias. *Merrill-Palmer Quarterly*, *19*, 21–39.

Nelson, K., & Ware, A. (2002). The reemergence of function. In N. L. Stein (Ed.), *Representation, memory, and development: Essays in honor of Jean Mandler* (pp. 161–184). Mahwah, NJ: Lawrence Erlbaum Associates, Inc.

Provasi, J., Dubon, C. D., & Bloch, H. (2001). Do 9-and 12-month-olds learn means–ends relation by observing? *Infant Behavior & Development*, *24*, 195–213.

Tomasello, M. (1999). *The cultural origins of human cognition*. Cambridge, MA: Harvard University Press.

Träuble, B., & Pauen, S. (in press). The role of functional information for infant categorization. *Cognition*. Manuscript submitted for publication.

Uzgiris, I. C. (1999). Imitation as activity: Developmental aspects. In J. Nadel & G. Butterworth (Eds.), *Imitation in infancy* (pp. 186–206). New York: Cambridge University Press.

EUROPEAN JOURNAL OF DEVELOPMENTAL PSYCHOLOGY
2007, 4 (1), 100–110

The directed attention model of infant social cognition

Vincent M. Reid
University of Leipzig and Max Planck Institute, Leipzig, Germany, and Durham University, UK

Tricia Striano
University of Leipzig and Max Planck Institute, Leipzig, Germany, and Vanderbilt University, Nashville, TN, USA

During infancy, humans have a limited attention span, a limited working memory and an initial lack of social experience. Given these constraints, why are infants so socially competent and how are they capable of processing such complex social information? Here we present an information-processing hypothesis that may account for these early social capacities. We outline those aspects of the social situation that must be processed for the infant to respond in a socially appropriate manner. We also outline potential cognitive sequences through which this information is processed. We conclude that the infant uses social information to determine what is relevant in the environment and in doing so, the infant uses each successive aspect of the social world to filter the overall amount of available information to a manageable size.

INTRODUCTION

Over the past twenty years, research into infant social-cognitive capacities has shown that they have some remarkable social abilities, such as the ability to imitate others, even during early infancy. Infant social

---

Correspondence should be addressed to Vincent M. Reid, Max Planck Institute for Human Cognitive and Brain Sciences, Stephanstraße 1a, 04103 Leipzig, Germany.
E-mail: reid@cbs.mpg.de or vincent.reid@durham.ac.uk

The authors are supported by the Sofja Kovalevskaja Award granted by the Alexander von Humboldt Foundation, donated by the German Federal Ministry of Education and Research, to TS.

We thank Melanie Demiral, Mariah Schug and Stefanie Hoehl for their comments on a draft of this paper.

DOI: 10.1080/17405620601005648

competencies are surprising given the complex, continuous and dynamic nature of other humans and their actions. Indeed, it has even been suggested that there are no environmental sources as complex as another person (Gallagher et al., 2000). The aim of this paper is to explain these skills while reconciling this with the infant's limited information-processing abilities.

Although models of social-cognitive processes have made important contributions to adult behavioural research on social-cognitive capacities (e.g., Chaiken & Trope, 1999), there have been few frameworks available for understanding early development. In fact, such models have been surprisingly absent from theorizing about the developmental bases of social perception. This may have been due to an initial need to map the parameters of infant abilities at different developmental stages before such models could be proposed. Alternatively, infant social cognitive capacities may have been interpreted in a wider and more established framework, such as Piaget's model of cognitive development (see, for example, the discussion of infant social-cognitive capacities in Anisfeld, 2005).

Adult models of social cognitive abilities have greatly informed research by providing new, testable hypotheses based on the rationale of the model. These hypotheses may not have been generated had not the model been applied. Two particular frameworks have come to the fore in adult research: dual-process models and social learning theory. First, dual-process models have been used whereby implicit and explicit processes are separated in terms of functional properties. The fundamental notion underlying these models is that some perceptual processes are rapid and require little effort, whereas others require concerted effort. For example, detecting someone's eye gaze is relatively automatic when compared with processing another person's motivations. Dual-process models are deliberately simplistic, however this is perhaps their strength (see, for example, Satpute & Lieberman, 2006, for a cognitive neuroscience perspective). An issue for developmental researchers is that these models do not consider how "implicit" operations may not be so automatic and simple to execute for an infant.

The second framework that has influenced social cognitive research with adults is social learning theory (SLT; Miller & Dollard, 1941). This theory, derived from behaviourism, is most often applied in clinical research (Bandura, 1977). It contains three basic notions. First, that human beings are evolutionarily designed for sensitivity to response consequences such as rewards or punishments. Second, that vicarious learning exists, whereby learning can occur by observing another person. Third, an individual is most likely to perform behaviours that the individual has observed performed by others with whom they identify. One primary drawback of SLT for developmental research is that the theory does not provide testable hypotheses in terms of developmental processes. Due to its behaviourist origins, it makes no distinction between an infant with a limited memory capacity and an adult with a wealth of experiences from which to draw contextual knowledge.

Infant working memory capacity has been shown to be relatively poor. This is in stark contrast to infant general capacities in the social domain. For example, Ross-Sheehy, Oakes, and Luck (2003) found that visual short-term memory rapidly changed over infancy, however skills by 13 months of age were still limited. In their preferential looking paradigm, infants viewed changing and nonchanging stimulus streams. Infants looked longer when they could recall the colours of the squares from the first presentation and if they changed in a subsequent presentation. Four- and six-month-olds only looked longer when a one-object stimulus stream changed colour. However by 10–13 months, infants could detect changes in displays with 2–3 items. When these capacities are compared with the number of components in a triadic interaction, there is clearly some form of differential processing occurring between those components of visual working memory and those cognitive processes involved in social situations. For instance, 3-month-old infants can process relations between themselves, an object and another person (Striano & Stahl, 2005). From an information-processing viewpoint, the social situation is clearly more complex than the task demands required in the visual working memory study.

In order to explain how infants exhibit complex social responses despite limited attentional resources and working memory capacities, we propose an information-processing account of how an infant may attend preferentially to key factors in the environment that are relevant for the social situation. This framework, termed the directed attention model, is based on known social-cognitive abilities of infants. For example, when posed with the question: "What needs to be processed in a social situation for socially appropriate responses to occur?", we can proceed to dissect the perceptual stages needed before the infant discerns enough of the environment in order to produce a socially correct behaviour.

We propose that the following key groupings of cognitive tasks must occur in order for the infant to successfully react to the social situation: (Stage One) the detection of socially relevant organisms; (Stage Two) the identification of socially relevant organisms; (Stage Three) assessment of the locus of attention and direction of eye gaze of the observed individual in relation to the infant; and (Stage Four) detection of any object-directed attention or object engagement by the observed individual. If these four components of the social situation are assessed, then the infant can: (Stage Five) infer the observed goal, and/or, prepare an appropriate response (e.g., establish contact, offer response, etc.). Each component will be briefly discussed, below, in terms of research into infant perceptual and cognitive abilities, together with how the model can explain infant social capacities at some ages.

STAGE ONE: THE DETECTION OF SOCIALLY RELEVANT ORGANISMS

The first thing that an infant needs to do in order to produce social responses is to detect those components of the environment that are socially relevant. Many studies have indicated that infants are sensitive to distinctions between animate and inanimate objects (e.g., Mandler & McDonough, 1996; Poulin-Dubois, Lepage, & Ferland, 1995). These studies suggest very early capacities to discriminate animate and inanimate objects in terms of the classification of motion, such as its regularity and energy source. Movement alone does not confer animacy.

Even though movement in peripheral regions of the visual field induces reflexive gaze orientation by humans, these cues can only tangentially assist in the detection of conspecifics. Many other aspects of the natural visual world move, such as most flora during a breeze. Infants must therefore be initially faced with the task of discerning movement that is biological from movement that is not biological.

The detection and interpretation of biological motion is critical for recognizing conspecifics (Bertenthal, Proffitt, & Kramer, 1987). Behavioural research suggests that humans detect and interpret biological motion very early in development, as shown by a preference to attend to biological motion when compared with stimuli depicting other forms of motion, such as randomly drifting dots. Much behavioural research has been conducted on infants' perception of biological motion, depicted by points of light moving as if attached to the major joints and the head of a moving person. Such stimuli, known as point-light displays (PLDs), convey little information regarding the schema of the underlying object or agent. Indeed, adult observers fail to report any relationship between static PLDs and the percept of a person. However, moving point-lights are perceived as depicting a human form in less than 0.5 seconds (Johansson, 1973). Three- and five-month-old infants discriminate these same moving point-light displays from ones in which the temporal patterning of the lights are perturbed. This is true even when the perturbation includes the same inter-relational mathematical vector translations as undisrupted PLDs (Bertenthal et al., 1987; Proffitt & Bertenthal, 1990).

It has been conjectured that multiple processing constraints, including stored knowledge of the human form, contribute to the interpretation of point-light displays throughout ontogeny (Bertenthal, 1993). This supposition is supported by findings indicating that 5-month-old infants do not discriminate point-light displays depicting unfamiliar agents, such as a four-legged spider, from a perturbed version (Bertenthal & Pinto, 1993). When combined, these studies indicate that experience of observing biological motion is required in order for infants to discriminate it from other forms of motion. Nonetheless, given that 3-month-olds have some capacity to discriminate biological motion from other types of motion, this suggests some very early capabilities. Furthermore, research investigating neural correlates to the perception of biological motion suggest that at least by 8 months, infants process at least some types of biological motion in a manner similar to adults at the neural level (Reid, Hoehl, & Striano, 2006). We consequently suggest that the detection of biological motion is of high importance for detecting conspecifics and that this process is required in order for the identification of the specifics of the social interaction.

STAGE TWO: THE IDENTIFICATION OF SOCIALLY RELEVANT ORGANISM

In our model, once the detection of biological motion has taken place, it would be beneficial to identify the specifics of the observed organism. This could occur as identification of species or an identification of an individual conspecific. Surprisingly, little work thus far has addressed the issue of infant sensitivity to human biological motion relative to biological motion produced by other species. However, much work has been conducted on how an infant discriminates between a familiar person, such as the mother, and an unfamiliar person. However, this research is almost exclusively focused on how infants process faces rather than how they discriminate the person—body and face inclusive—as a whole relative to another person. Even though an extensive review of this literature is not in the scope of this article, we will briefly summarize some key findings.

Perhaps most importantly, newborn infants can discern individual people and differences between people. Utilizing a preferential looking paradigm, Bushnell, Sai, and Mullin (1989) found that even a few hours after birth, newborn infants preferentially attended to their mother's face. It has been proposed that this early capacity to identify individuals is not the same as that possessed by adult humans, with the possibility that subcortical mechanisms are utilized before 3 months of age, whereas cortical regions process this information at later ages (Nelson, 2001). The early mechanism is conjectured to be less adaptable in terms of reconciling new visual information with previously stored representations.

Electrophysiological work with older infants suggests some capacities to discriminate familiar and novel people. de Haan and Nelson (1999) presented 6-month-old infants with a photograph of their mother and a stranger and with familiar and unfamiliar objects. They showed evidence for a familiarity effect. The resultant event-related potential negative component (Nc) was larger in amplitude for familiar faces than that for unfamiliar faces. Subsequent research into the functional properties of the Nc suggests that it is a robust index of infant attention (Richards, 2003). The results of de Haan and Nelson (1999) therefore suggest differential processing of familiar and unfamiliar conspecifics as well as suggesting an increased allocation of attentional resources when viewing familiar faces. As the Nc is maximal in amplitude at around 400 milliseconds, this suggests rapid encoding of key components of the human face in order to discriminate familiar from unfamiliar people.

STAGE THREE: ASSESSMENT OF THE LOCUS OF ATTENTION

Once the detection and identification of an organism has occurred, we speculate that the observing infant will attend towards characteristics that index the locus of attention of the observed organism. In the human face, this can be detected by observing the orientation of the eyes (Farroni, Csibra, Simeon, & Johnson, 2002) and the orientation of the head coupled with the orientation of the eyes (see Farroni, Johnson, & Csibra, 2004). Research into how infants determine the orientation of the entire human body has not been investigated. This is most likely due to the need to reduce the number of variables involved for an effective experimental design. However, we contend that if the observed individual is not oriented towards the infant, then it is likely that the individual is not intending to engage with the infant in a social manner and that this will be detected by the infant. Interestingly, once interaction has been established, then brief breaks in mutual gaze do not appear to influence the infant's understanding of a mutually enabled interaction (Nadel, Carchon, Kervella, Marcelli, & Réserbat-Plantey, 1999). This underlines the point that infants are highly predisposed to communicate, reciprocate and connect with other people (Striano, 2004; Trevarthen, 1979).

The human infant's discriminative abilities are highly robust with respect to elements of the human face that delineate the locus of attention. For example, Farroni et al. (2002) showed that newborn infants can discriminate between a face with eyes oriented towards the infant and eyes oriented away from the infant. These authors also demonstrated that 4-month-old infants differentially process faces with direct vs. averted gaze and that this is processed rapidly (c. 250 ms) after faces are presented to infants.

A first step in successful communication is understanding when a social signal is directed at and intended for the self. In adulthood, specialized brain regions activate when a social signal is detected. When an adult hears their name or are the visual target of someone's direct gaze, the paracingulate cortex and temporal poles activate (Kampe, Frith, Dolan, & Frith, 2001). Regardless of modality (auditory or visual) the adult brain is ready to detect another's intention to communicate. Newborns are sensitive to faces, voices, and eye contact (Rochat & Striano, 1999), but do not appear to have particular social expectations or show reduced attention or affect towards a social partner who suddenly stops interacting. However, with only six weeks of interactive experience infants show a classic still-face effect (Bertin & Striano, 2006). They reduce their smiling and gazing and then attempt to re-engage the social partner when suddenly still. Also by this age, infants distinguish between an adult who interacts in a relevant way by providing contingent feedback such as smiles and vocalizations compared to someone who interacts in an irregular way, with delayed social feedback (Striano, Henning, & Stahl, 2005).

These studies summarized here suggest robust social capacities in the domain of determining the locus of another's attention. Should the infant process this information, further socially relevant components of the environment can be determined. Through removing elements of the environment that are not socially relevant, the infant has effectively filtered extraneous information, thereby enhancing the chance of a correct discrimination of further components of the social situation.

STAGE FOUR: DETECTION OF OBJECT DIRECTED ATTENTION

Recent studies into eye gaze cuing and object processing suggest an early capacity for discerning a relationship between a person and an object. In one study, 4-month-old infants watched a video presentation of an adult gazing toward one of two objects. When presented with the same objects a second time, infants gazed toward the uncued object significantly more—suggesting that it was more novel (Reid & Striano, 2005). This suggests that 4-month-old infants not only followed the gaze of the adult, but acquired information about the object that was the focus on the adult's attention. In one study investigating the neural correlates of observing eye gaze on object processing, infants viewed an adult's face on-screen, and the eyes of the adult gazed toward an object. In the test trials, infants viewed the objects a second time. Infants exhibited enhanced neural processing (indexed by an enhanced positive slow wave) of the uncued object during test trials (Reid, Striano, Kaufman, & Johnson, 2004). Thus, the cued object was more highly processed when the face and object were on the screen and was subsequently more familiar to the infant when presented a second time than the uncued object.

The results of these experiments suggest that by 4 months of age infants use the gaze of an adult to facilitate attention to a location. This in turn biases processing of information from that location relative to objects in other locations. Objects in uncued locations are therefore inherently more novel for infants than objects in cued locations. In recent research investigating the neural correlates of joint attention in 9-month-old infants, it has been shown that infants allocate significantly more attentional resources to objects that are the subject of joint attention interactions relative to objects that are not involved in joint attention situations (Striano, Reid, & Hoehl, 2006). This result suggests that infants increase attention to aspects of the environment that are more socially salient.

These results are perhaps the most compelling support for the directed attention model of infant social cognition. These data demonstrate that infants use others as tools with which to reduce the amount of information available for them to process in the surrounding world. To this extent, they fit very well with the notion that infants direct their limited attentional resources and memory capacity to components of the world that are important for social relations.

STAGE FIVE: INFERENCE OF GOALS AND/OR PREPARE RESPONSE

Infants are capable of detecting and identifying others. They also have skills at remarkably early ages in determining the locus of another person's attention as well as their relationship to external components of the world, such as objects or locations. However, the ability to infer goals appears not to develop until the beginning of the second half of the first postnatal year. We suggest that infants are capable of processing intentions and goals only when earlier perceptual processes of the social environment have been resolved.

Much research suggests that markers of intentionality throughout human action may be critical to understanding goal direction. At least by 9 months infants are capable of discerning intentional from accidental action (Woodward, 1999). Research also suggests that by 9 months of age infants can understand action in terms of future goals and the efficient means to achieve these goals (Csibra, Gergely, Biró, Koós, & Brockbank, 1999), with more recent evidence suggesting this skill is evident by 6 months (Kamewrai, Kato, Kanda, Ishiguro, & Hiraki, 2005). These studies also suggest that infants do not require the presentation of the end-state of an action in order to attribute a goal to an action. Other work suggests that infants of 9 months focus on the goals of an action over other components, such as the direction of the movement (Woodward, 2003).

One important issue is the reason for why younger infants fail to detect intentions from other forms of human action. It may well be that the number of variables that are required to be maintained in working memory produce the inability to detect goal directed action in younger ages. Literally, there is too much information to maintain and therefore the processing of additional information, in this case information pertaining to goal directions, will suffer. The directed attention model can account for this in terms of overloaded working memory capacities. For example, the directed attention model would predict that a young infant would be able to maintain information about one agent displaying a different emotional stance towards two objects, whereas two agents each displaying a separate emotional expression towards one object may be an observed social situation that is too complex for an infant to process. This is particularly that case if other components of the social situation take precedence in terms of infant attention. For example, it is more socially important to determine the locus of an observed individual's attention in relation to the self than it is to identify the goal of the observed individual. There is, however, an overall caveat that much further work is required with younger infants in order to map the developmental trajectory of discerning intentions and detecting goals.

It is also possible that infants may produce a response at this stage in determining the parameters of the social situation. This may be due to the infant discerning enough information at this point in processing the situation to produce a socially correct response in the majority of settings. Potentially, the detection of goals is not required in many social situations in order for an infant to produce a valid social response.

CONCLUSIONS

We hope that this model can provide a framework in terms of information processing for understanding social-cognitive skills throughout infancy. For example, the directed attention model predicts that the addition of biological motion to more complex aspects of the social environment, such as normal and disrupted human body schema, may help facilitate detection of aspects of body schema that would not otherwise be attended to. The discrimination of possible and impossible body schema may be a likely experimental outcome, which cannot be discriminated by infants using static stimuli.

One caveat of the directed attention model is that this is a purely perceptual account of how infants successfully process social information. The infant's role in this model is entirely passive. In the real world, infants are highly interactive in their initiation of, and involvement in, social interactions. This will of course change the order of the cognitive sequence in the model. However, the individual components of detecting others and determining their direction of attention will likely not change.

The directed attention model also has implications for general learning mechanisms throughout infancy. For example, learning to determine the referent of a novel word is an intrinsically social act, as is learning to speak (see Baldwin & Moses, 2001). Application of the directed attention model to these social situations may predict the success of a given infant at these tasks due to the dynamics of the specific social situation.

This is the first attempt to produce a model integrating social capacities in infancy with known cognitive skills. To the extent that use of this interpretative framework may generate new hypotheses, it is hoped that this simple model proves a useful tool in future research in early social cognition.

REFERENCES

Anisfeld, M. (2005). No compelling evidence to dispute Piaget's timetable of the development of representational imitation in infancy. In S. Hurley & N. Chater (Eds.), *Perspectives on imitation: From cognitive neuroscience to social science* (pp. 107–133). Cambridge, MA: MIT Press.

Baldwin, D. A., & Moses, L. J. (2001). Links between social understanding and early word learning: Challenges to current accounts. *Social Development*, *10*(3), 309–329.

Bandura, A. (1977). *Social learning theory*. Englewood Cliffs, NJ: Prentice Hall.

Bertenthal, B. I. (1993). Infants' perception of biomechanical motions: Intrinsic image and knowledge-based constraints. In C. Granrud (Ed.), *Visual perception and cognition in infancy* (pp. 175–214). Hillsdale, NJ: Lawrence Erlbaum Associates, Inc.

Bertenthal, B. I., & Pinto, J. (1993). Dynamical constraints in the perception and production of human movements. In M. Gunnar & E. Thelen (Eds.), *The Minnesota symposia on child psychology: Systems in development* (pp. 209–239). Hillsdale, NJ: Lawrence Erlbaum Associates, Inc.

Bertenthal, B. I., Proffitt, D. R., & Kramer, S. J. (1987). The perception of biomechanical motions by infants: Implementation of various processing constraints. *Journal of Experimental Psychology: Human Perception and Performance*, *13*, 577–585.

Bertin, E., & Striano, T. (2006). The still-face response in newborn, 1.5-, and 3-month-old infants. *Infant Behavior & Development*, *29*, 294–297.

Bushnell, I. W. R., Sai, F., & Mullin, J. T. (1989). Neonatal recognition of the mother's face. *British Journal of Developmental Psychology*, *7*, 3–15.

Chaiken, S., & Trope, Y. (Eds.). (1999). *Dual-process theories in social psychology*. New York: Guilford Press.

Csibra, G., Gergely, G., Biró, S., Koós, O., & Brockbank, M. (1999). Goal attribution without agency cues: The perception of 'pure reason' in infancy. *Cognition*, *72*, 237–267.

de Haan, M., & Nelson, C. A. (1999). Brain activity differentiates face and object processing in 6-month-old infants. *Developmental Psychology*, *35*, 1113–1121.

Farroni, T., Csibra, G., Simeon, F., & Johnson, M. H. (2002). Eye contact detection in humans from birth. *Proceedings of the National Academy of Sciences*, *99*, 9602–9605.

Farroni, T., Johnson, M. H., & Csibra, G. (2004). Mechanisms of eye gaze perception during infancy. *Journal of Cognitive Neuroscience*, *16*, 1320–1326.

Gallagher, H. L., Happé, F., Brunswick, N., Fletcher, P. C., Frith, U., & Frith, C. D. (2000). Reading the mind in cartoons and stories: An fMRI study of "theory of mind" in verbal and nonverbal tasks. *Neuropsychologia*, *38*, 11–21.

Johansson, G. (1973). Visual perception of biological motion and a model for its analysis. *Perception & Psychophysics*, *14*, 201–211.

Kamewrai, K., Kato, M., Kanda, T., Ishiguro, H., & Hiraki, K. (2005). Six-and-a-half-month-old children positively attribute goals to human action and to humanoid-robot motion. *Cognitive Development*, *20*, 303–320.

Kampe, K. K., Frith, C. D., Dolan, R. J., & Frith, U. (2001). Reward value of attractiveness and gaze. *Nature*, *413*(6856), 589.

Mandler, J. M., & McDonough, L. (1996). Drinking and driving don't mix: Inductive generalisation in infancy. *Cognition, 59*, 307–335.

Miller, N., & Dollard, J. (1941). *Social learning and imitation.* New Haven, CT: Yale University Press.

Nadel, J., Carchon, I., Kervella, C., Marcelli, D., & Réserbat-Plantey, D. (1999). Expectancies for social contingency in 2-month-olds. *Developmental Science, 2*, 164–173.

Nelson, C. A. (2001). The development and neural bases of face recognition. *Infant and Child Development, 10*, 3–18.

Poulin-Dobois, D., Lepage, A., & Ferland, D. (1996). Infants' concept of animacy. *Cognitive Development, 11*, 19–36.

Proffitt, D. R., & Bertenthal, B. I. (1990). Converging operations revisited: Assessing what infants perceive using discrimination measures. *Perception and Psychophysics, 41*, 1–12.

Reid, V., & Striano, T. (2005). Adult gaze influences infant attention and object processing implications for cognitive neuroscience. *European Journal of Neuroscience, 21*, 1763–1766.

Reid, V. M., Hoehl, S., & Striano, T. (2006). The perception of biological motion by infants: An event-related potential study. *Neuroscience Letters, 395*, 211–214.

Reid, V. M., Striano, T., Kaufman, J., & Johnson, M. (2004). Eye gaze cuing facilitates neural processing of objects in 4 month old infants. *Neuroreport, 15*, 2553–2556.

Richards, J. E. (2003). Attention affects the recognition of briefly presented visual stimuli in infants: An ERP study. *Developmental Science, 6*, 312–328.

Rochat, P., & Striano, T. (1999). Social cognitive development in the first year. In P. Rochat (Ed.), *Early social cognition* (pp. 3–34). Hillsdale, NJ: Lawrence Erlbaum Associates, Inc.

Ross-Shirley, A., Oakes, L. M., & Luck, S. J. (2003). The development of visual short-term memory capacity in infants. *Child Development, 74*(6), 1807–1822.

Satpute, A. B., & Lieberman, M. D. (2006). Integrating automatic and controlled processing into neurocognitive models of social cognition. *Brain Research, 1079*, 86–97.

Striano, T. (2004). Direction of regard and the still-face effect in the first year: Does intention matter? *Child Development, 75*(2), 468–479.

Striano, T., Henning, A., & Stahl, D. (2005). Sensitivity to social contingencies between 1 and 3 months of age. *Developmental Science, 8*(6), 509–519.

Striano, T., Reid, V. M., & Hoehl, S. (2006). Neural mechanisms of joint attention in infancy. *European Journal of Neuroscience, 23*, 2819–2823.

Striano, T., & Stahl, D. (2005). Sensitivity to triadic attention in early infancy. *Developmental Science, 4*, 333–343.

Trevarthen, C. (1979). Communication and co-operation in early infancy: A description of primary intersubjectivity. In M. Bullowa (Ed.), *Before speech: The beginning of interpersonal communication* (pp. 321–347). Cambridge, UK: Cambridge University Press.

Woodward, A. (1999). Infants' ability to distinguish between purposeful and non-purposeful behaviors. *Infant Behaviour & Development, 22*(2), 145–160.

Woodward, A. L. (2003). Infants' developing understanding of the link between looker and object. *Developmental Science, 6*(3), 297–311.

EUROPEAN JOURNAL OF DEVELOPMENTAL PSYCHOLOGY
2007, 4 (1), 111–125

Infant perception of the relative relevance of different manual actions

Bianca Jovanovic and Gudrun Schwarzer
University of Giessen, Germany

Six- to nine-month-olds have been found to perceive manual actions as object-directed. They apply this interpretation even to unfamiliar, non-purposeful-looking movements if these produce salient object-directed effects. We investigated whether infants engage in a differential weighting of movement–effect instances, perceiving some instances as more "meaningful" than others. Thus, infants might preferentially encode movement–effect couplings involving prehensile movements, in contrast to couplings involving movements like touching, even if these produce salient effects. Seven- and nine-month-olds were habituated to two movement–effect couplings in close succession, a grasp/lift event and a touch/overthrow event, each directed at one of two objects, respectively. Subsequently, one object was exchanged, and looking time to the same events, with one of them involving the novel object, was measured. Preferential encoding of the prehensile action should result in a stronger dishabituation to a change in the object involved in this action (primary object) than to a change in the object involved in the touch/overthrow event (secondary object). Nine-month-olds looked significantly longer at a primary-object change. Seven-month-olds tended to look longer at the secondary-object change. This suggests that a preferential encoding of "meaningful" as compared to salient events develops between 7 and 9 months.

INTRODUCTION

The development of the ability to interpret and predict human action and the mechanisms underlying this ability have been within the focus of

Correspondence should be addressed to Bianca Jovanovic, University of Giessen, FB 06, Otto-Behaghel-Str. 10/F1, D-35394 Giessen, Germany.
E-mail: Bianca.Jovanovic@psychol.uni-giessen.de

We would like to thank Knut Drewing for many helpful comments on the manuscript. Further, we thank the research team for helping to conduct the experiments, especially Dominique Rompf and Katinka Bloemer. Finally, we thank the parents and infants who so generously donated their time and energy to participate in this study.

DOI: 10.1080/17405620601033186

developmental research during the past two decades. Recently, researchers have begun to identify candidates for primitive precursors of more complex action understanding even in infants (e.g., Csibra, Gergely, Bíró, Koós, & Brockbank, 1999; Gergely, Nádasdy, Csibra, & Bíró, 1995; Woodward, 1998, 1999). The most basic aspect of an action, distinguishing an action from a mere movement, is its goal-directedness. This means that an action is always directed at producing some intended end-state, like for example reaching out and grasping an object. Already infants seem to possess a corresponding rudimentary understanding of goal-directedness, which is reflected in the capacity to form simple representations of observed manual actions by linking movements with the objects they are directed at (e.g., Woodward, 1998). However, such early knowledge is rudimentary in the sense that it is probably limited to the perceivable features of the action and need not encompass assumptions about the underlying intentions. In order to accentuate this difference, this kind of knowledge has been termed an understanding of object-directedness (Wellman & Phillips, 2001). Developmental studies have just begun to specify the conditions under which infants regard movements as object-directed (e. g. Király, Jovanovic, Prinz, Aschersleben, & Gergely, 2003; Woodward, 1998). In particular, the perception of object-directedness has been found to be enhanced when the respective movement produces an effect on the object, even when the movement looks non-purposeful to adults (Jovanovic, 2003; Jovanovic et al., submitted; Király et al., 2003). The concept of "action effects" refers to the perceivable consequences a movement exerts on a specific object, such as a change of state in the object. The present work seeks to extend our knowledge about early action perception by examining whether and when infants engage in a differential weighting of different movement–effect combinations. Before introducing the paradigm employed in the present study, we give a brief overview of studies on the development of the perception of goal-directed actions and, specifically, manual actions, which form the background to the current study.

Perception of goal-directed actions

Focusing on the developing ability to analyse instrumental actions in terms of their goal-related properties, one set of studies has investigated when infants start to infer the unfulfilled goals of simple actions. It was found that 15- and 18-month-olds (Johnson, Booth, & O'Hearn, 2001; Meltzoff, 1995), who observed a model try but fail to complete different object-directed actions, completed the actions when given the opportunity to imitate, instead of just copying the surface features of the failed attempts. In 12-month-olds, this result was however not found (Bellagamba & Tomasello, 1999). As they were able to reproduce the same actions when these were fully modelled, including the end-state, their failure cannot be attributed to difficulties in producing the motor acts, but seems to be conceptual in nature. In sum, this indicates that children begin to understand intended action effects as separate from actual movement effects, or at least to anticipate possible outcomes, in the second year of life. Furthermore, by 14 months, children differentially imitate perceptually identical intended and accidental acts that can only be distinguished on the basis of verbal comments (Carpenter, Akhtar, & Tomasello, 1998). Thus, infants' reasoning by this age takes into account factors that go beyond simple action analysis. Other studies employing the looking-time paradigm suggest that already 9-month-old infants understand something about the "rationality" of actions. Infants watching abstract entities moving towards a goal displayed sensitivity for the most efficient movement path, thereby taking contextual constraints into account (Csibra et al., 1999; Gergely et al., 1995). With human or human-like agents, even 6.5-month-olds show evidence of such understanding (Kamewari, Kato, Kanda, Ishiguro, & Hiraki, 2005).

A necessary precondition for the ability to predict and evaluate possible outcomes of people's actions is being able to represent the basic elements of object-directed actions and their relations, that is, object-directed movements, objects and their interaction. This knowledge manifests itself in infants' looking responses to simple object-directed manual actions.

Perception of manual actions

Rudimentary action understanding in 6- to 9-month-olds, and in one study even in 5-month-olds, has been documented in habituation studies (Hofer, Hauf, & Aschersleben, 2005; Király et al., 2003; Woodward, 1999) employing a paradigm originally introduced by Woodward (1998). In the original study, infants were habituated to a grasping action directed at one of two objects, performed by a hidden actor. Subsequently, the positions of the objects were switched. In one test condition, the grasping act was directed at the old object that now occupied a new position and thus afforded a change in movement direction. In a different test condition, the goal object changed, as now the alternative object was grasped, while the movement remained directed at the same position as before. A selectively stronger dishabituation to the change in goal object as opposed to the change in movement direction was taken to indicate that infants had perceived a relation between the movement and the specific object at which it was directed. A corresponding preferential encoding of the goal object was found when grasping acts were presented, it could not, however, be replicated when infants watched other, unfamiliar, movements such as a hand dropping backwards onto an object (Woodward, 1999). Furthermore, when an agent proximally points to an object, touching it with his finger, it is only by 12 months that infants understand this movement as object-directed (Woodward & Guajardo, 2002). Thus, the establishment of contact does not seem to be a sufficient cue for object-directedness. Subsequent studies (Jovanovic, 2003; Jovanovic et al., submitted; Király et al., 2003) demonstrated that a more relevant factor could be the occurrence of object-directed effects, which were absent in the original studies. Employing the Woodward paradigm, these authors showed that 6- and 9-month-old infants are able to link an unfamiliar movement to an object if the movement produces a salient object-directed effect, as in this case a displacement of the object. This suggests that in order to understand that a movement is directed at a specific object, infants have to experience that something is done to the object: they have to be given evidence of a functional relation. Importantly, this even works when the movement looks non-purposeful to the adult observer, such as the dropping of the back of a person's hand onto an object as described above. One interpretation of these data could be that infants, unlike adults, regard any movement that terminates on an object and is associated with a salient effect as object-directed, and make no distinction between purposeful and non-purposeful actions on the basis of perceptual cues. A different possibility is that infants, although lacking the concept of a "purposeful" action, might still perceive some movement–effect combinations as more meaningful than others. In other terms, not all movement–effect combinations might be equally appropriate for infants to establish a link between movement and object. The extant studies, however, do not allow for a distinction between these two possibilities, as none of them directly compares the encoding of different movement–effect combinations within the same context. The present study focuses on this issue by studying infants' perception of simple object-directed manual actions and comparing the encoding of objects under different conditions of movement–effect couplings.

Which sort of movement–effect coupling could be of particular importance? One possibility is that particularly frequently encountered couplings are preferentially encoded (see also Woodward, Sommerville, & Guajardo, 2001). One of the prime candidates for an especially relevant movement–effect coupling would be a prehensile movement like grasping, associated with an effect, like for example lifting. Already 4-month-old infants conceive of basic aspects of grasping actions (Leslie, 1984). Furthermore, infants observe such a movement very frequently. Evidence in favour of a role of experience for infants' action understanding comes from a study by Sommerville, Woodward, and Needham (2005), in which 3-month-olds who were initially not able to grasp, but were given the opportunity of gaining action experience by wearing "sticky mittens", were more likely to perceive another person's grasp as object-directed than infants who were not given this opportunity. Over and above the impact of own agentive experience, differential exposure to different action–effect couplings might also lead infants to encode particular couplings as more meaningful or more relevant than others. We therefore expected that infants would regard a prehensile movement associated with an effect, like grasping an object and lifting it, as more relevant than a non-prehensile movement involving a salient effect, like touching an object and thereby overthrowing it. To test this hypothesis, we investigated 7- and 9-month-old infants' encoding of two different target objects during an event where two movements resulted in two different effects on the two objects. Specifically, we habituated infants to a video displaying a hand reaching toward one of two objects positioned on a stage. The hand entered the screen from one side, grasped the toy at the farther end ("primary object") and lifted it. Importantly, during the reaching movement, the hand touched the second object ("secondary object") and overthrew it. After habituation, infants were presented with the same procedure, except that one of the objects—either the primary or the secondary object—had been exchanged for a novel object. In line with our argumentation we expected infants to dishabituate more strongly to a change in the primary object than to a change in the secondary object. As extant studies point to an emerging understanding of goal-directedness at around 6 months, we chose slightly older, that is 7- and 9-month-old infants for our study, in order to capture a time window in which this understanding can be expected to be more or less firmly established. Furthermore, the age of 9 months has been deemed a time involving crucial changes in infants' social understanding by some researchers (e.g., Tomasello, 1999), which marks it as an especially interesting period to look at.

METHOD

Participants

Forty-eight infants, 24 9-month-olds and 24 7-month-olds participated in the final sample. Infants were recruited by obtaining their birth records from local municipal councils of the Giessen area and neighbouring communities and contacting their parents by mail or by word of mouth. Signed consent was obtained from the parents before each experimental session. In the 9-month sample 8 male and 16 female subjects participated, mean age being 9 months 19 days (range: 8;30–9;30). Seven additional infants were invited but did not complete the procedure due to fussiness. Eight infants did not reach the habituation criterion (see procedure section) and were thus excluded from the sample.

In the 7-month sample 13 male and 11 female subjects participated, mean age being 6 months 30 days (range: 6;09 – 8;03). Six additional infants were invited but did not complete the procedure due to fussiness. Nine infants did not reach the habituation criterion (see procedure section) and were thus excluded from the sample.

Apparatus

The experiment took place in a rectangular cabin with one open side, designed to accommodate a caregiver sitting on a chair with the child on her lap. Infants were seated on their caregiver's lap at a distance of approximately 60 cm from the stage. A 17″ monitor inserted in the rear wall of the cabin was used to present the videos. The presentation was run on a computer with a split desktop—one for the presentation and one for the control of the videos- and was controlled by a collaborator sitting behind the cabin, who activated the respective video clips from a playlist of a common video player interface. A second collaborator stood behind the cabin, observed the infants through a peep-hole and coded looking times on-line. A camera positioned behind another peephole in the rear wall of the cabin yielded an on-line close-up view of the infants that was registered and subsequently used for reliability measurement.

Stimuli and design

Stimuli consisted of different video clips displaying hand actions towards different objects. The objects were placed on the left and right side of a stage against a black background (see Figure 1). They were common multi-coloured plastic toys: one telephone-shaped toy, one narrow cylindrical toy and one broad hexagonal toy. All toys were filled with beads or similar materials and made different characteristic noises when overthrown.

Each video clip started with a short black frame and a concurrent orientation sound, which served to draw infants' attention to the display. Subsequently, infants were shown three types of videos in succession: the habituation video, a familiarization video and a test video.

Habituation video. In the habituation video, infants were presented with a scene in which a hand entered either from the left or the right side of the screen and moved to the contralateral side towards one of the objects. On the way to that object the hand touched the other object standing in its motion path and overthrew it. While the object was falling, the hand continued on its path until it grasped the object on the other side and lifted it. The falling event was accompanied by a salient rattling sound, while the lifting event was soundless.

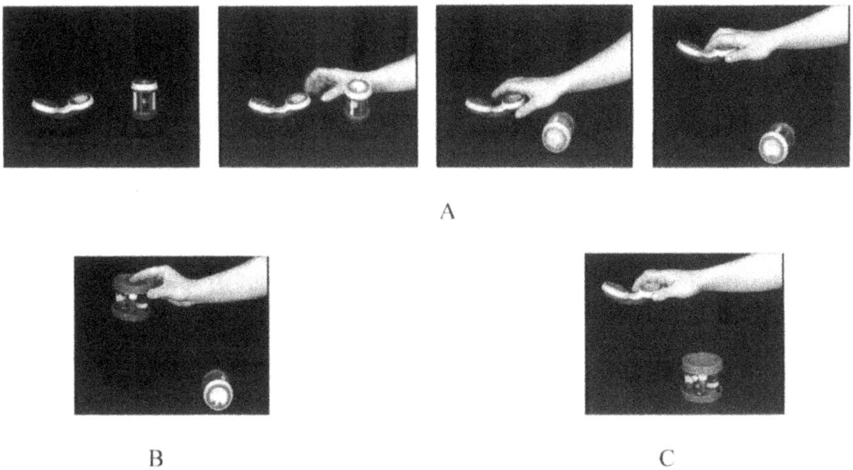

Figure 1. (A) Habituation clip; (B) Last frame of an exemplary "primary object change" event; (C) Last frame of an exemplary "secondary object change" event.

Accordingly, there were two types of roles for the objects involved in the habituation event. An object could either be the *primary object*. In this case it was the object that was grasped and lifted. In the second case, an object could be the *secondary object*, which was the object that was overthrown and fell down. The telephone-shaped toy and the cylindrical toy always served as either the *primary toy*—the toy that was grasped—or the *secondary toy*—the toy that was overthrown—and their use in either of the roles was counterbalanced.

Familiarization video. Following habituation, infants were presented with a familiarization video that served to show infants that one of the objects, either the primary or the secondary object, had been exchanged for a novel object. It was always the hexagonal toy that served as the *novel toy*. During this trial, no action took place and no arm was visible.

Test video. In the following test video, the identity of the objects remained the same as in the familiarization trial, but now the arm reappeared and performed the same action as in the habituation video. In the *primary object change condition*, the hand grasped and lifted the new toy occupying the same position as the primary object before, while the secondary object that was overthrown remained the same. In the *secondary object change condition*, the hand threw over the new toy occupying the same position as the secondary object before, while the primary object that was grasped and lifted remained the same.

All videos ended with a still frame depicting the final scene, which remained activated for as long as infants continued to look at it.

In all conditions, the objects occupied the same positions (the telephone was always placed left and the cylinder right), while the direction from which the hand entered the screen depended on which object was assigned the role of the "primary", i.e., grasped, object and which object was assigned the role of the "secondary" object.

All videos lasted 4 seconds and care was taken that analogous segments of the different clips, such as the time before movement initiation, subtended equally long time durations.

Procedure

Each infant was tested individually. At the beginning of each session, infants were seated on their caregivers' laps. In order to minimize interference by the parents, they were instructed to close their eyes and refrain from interacting with their children throughout the presentation.

During habituation infants were repeatedly presented with the habituation video described in the stimuli section. Infants' looking times were measured on-line by a trained observer who watched the child through a peep-hole in the rear of the cabin and depressed a computer key when the child was looking at the monitor and released the key when the child looked away. The looking times and the habituation criterion were automatically calculated by a custom-made computer program. Looking times were counted from the moment the action started until the child averted his or her gaze for at least 2 seconds. As described above, after the completion of the video, the final frame remained activated as a still picture for as long as infants continued to look at the scene. Maximum trial length was set at 60 seconds. If the infant exceeded this time, the trial finished automatically and the next trial was initiated.

The presentation of the videos was thus dependent on infants' reactions and habituation was determined in an infant-control fashion. The criterion was computed relative to the first three trials that added to at least 12 seconds, and was reached when infants' total looking times during three additional consecutive trials decreased to at least 50% of the three critical trials. At minimum, infants were presented with 6 trials; the maximal number of presentations was 14 trials. Children who did not habituate within this range were excluded from the sample.

After habituation, infants were shown one familiarization trial depicting a new configuration of objects, in which either the primary or the secondary object was exchanged for a novel object, depending on the test condition. In the subsequent test trial, infants were presented with one of the test films, as described in the stimulus session. In order to avoid confusing infants with three different toys continuously changing positions and roles, test conditions were presented to independent samples, so that each child either saw a primary object change event or a secondary object change event during the test.

The variation of the identity of the *primary object* (telephone/cylinder) and the type of *test condition* (primary object change/secondary object change) resulted in 4 conditions.

Twelve infants of each age group were randomly assigned to the two test conditions (primary object change vs secondary object change, see procedure section). In case of the object, in the 9-month-group infants were evenly distributed across conditions, while in the 7-month-group 14 infants were presented with the telephone in the role of the primary object and 10 infants were presented with the cylinder as primary object.

Reliability analysis and data coding

Looking times were coded on-line by a live coder and then re-coded by a second coder from video tapes. Inter-observer reliability, computed by correlating the fixation times recorded by each observer on each trial for a single infant, and subsequently averaging across infants, exceeded .9.

RESULTS

To reduce positive skew, looking times were subjected to a natural logarithmic transformation prior to data analysis. In a first step, preliminary analyses for the factors primary object (telephone vs cylinder) and sex were conducted on the habituation data and on test data. As the analyses yielded no significant effects, data were collapsed across these variables for the subsequent analyses.

In a second step, we took a closer look at the habituation data. An analysis with habituation (first two trials vs last two trials) as within-subject variable and age-group (7- vs 9-month-olds) and test condition (primary object change vs secondary object change) as between-subjects variables revealed a significant main effect of habituation, $F(1, 44) = 192.74$; $p < .001$, indicating a significant decline of looking times over time (first two trials: $M = 36.76$, $SD = 6.86$; last two trials: $M = 14.80$, $SD = 8.05$), as expected by the habituation criterion. There were no significant effects involving test condition (all Fs < 1). Further, there was a significant interaction between habituation and age-group, $F(1, 44) = 6.77$; $p < .05$, indicating a stronger decline of looking times in the 9-month group (first two trials: $M = 34.33$, $SD = 14.0$; last two trials: $M = 11.58$, $SD = 6.12$) than in the 7-month group (first two trials: $M = 39.19$, $SD = 19.31$; last two trials: $M = 18.0$, $SD = 8.58$), and a significant main effect of age-group, originating from overall higher looking times in the younger group as compared to the older group. However, a corresponding difference in processing of the events was not reflected in the mean number of habituation trials. Interestingly, in this case 7-month-olds needed a lower number of trials to habituate ($M = 8.25$) than the 9-month-olds ($M = 9.66$). Statistically, however, this difference failed to reach significance, $F(1, 46) = 3.28$; $p > .05$. Separate analyses for the two age-groups yielded highly significant main effects of habituation in both groups, 7-month-olds: $F(1, 22) = 57.02$; $p < .001$; 9-month-olds: $F(1, 22) = 153.73$; $p < .001$, and, importantly, again no significant main effects or interactions involving condition (all Fs < 1). Thus, the groups allocated to the two test conditions did not differ systematically in how they encoded the presented events.

To test our hypothesis, we conducted a mixed-model analysis of variance (ANOVA) with trial type (last habituation trial vs test-trial) as within-subjects variable and test condition (primary object change vs secondary object change) and age-group (7 months vs 9 months) as between-subjects variables. The analysis revealed a significant main effect of trial type, $F(1, 44) = 10.9$; $p = .002$, indicating an overall increase in looking time from habituation to test and a significant main effect of age-group, $F(1, 44) = 5.67$; $p < .05$, indicating higher overall looking times in the group of 7-month-olds. However, there was no main effect of test condition ($F < 1$), which indicates that overall looking times were at the same level independent of condition. The interaction between test trial and test condition, which was of special interest for this study, failed to reach significance, $F(1, 44) = 2.77$; $p > .10$, however this interaction was qualified by a significant 3-way interaction between trial type, test-condition and age-group, $F(1, 44) = 5.63$; $p < .05$, indicating that the two age-groups dishabituated differently to the two test conditions (see Figures 2 and 3).

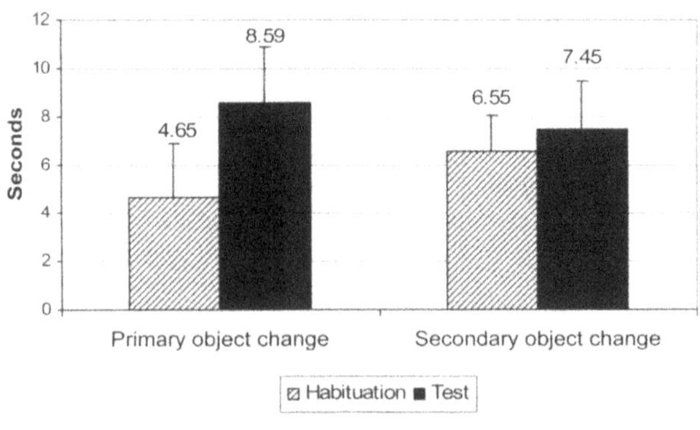

Figure 2. Mean looking times during the last habituation trials and the test trials of the two conditions in the 9-month sample.

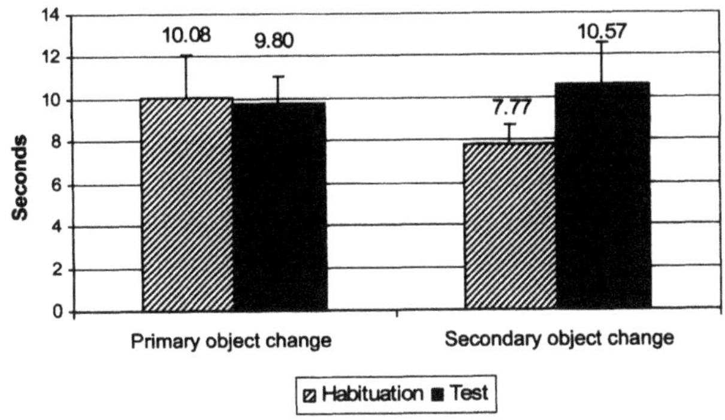

Figure 3. Mean looking times during the last habituation trials and the test trials of the two conditions in the 7-month sample.

In order to further examine this difference, we conducted separate analyses for the two age-groups. As regards the 7-month-olds, a mixed-model ANOVA revealed a main effect of trial type, $F(1, 22) = 4.78$; $p < .05$, but no interaction between trial type and test condition ($F < 1$). A different picture emerged from the analysis of the 9-month-olds' data: here, we found both a significant main effect of trial type, $F(1, 22) = 6.25$; $p < .05$, and a significant interaction between trial type and test condition, $F(1, 22) = 6.05$; $p < .05$. This interaction was due to infants' longer looking times to a change in the primary object as compared to a change in the secondary object, and is in line with our predictions (see Figure 2). Simple t-tests examining the difference between looking times in habituation and test trials conducted for both samples furthermore yielded a clearer picture. Whereas the 9-month-olds clearly differentiated between habituation and primary object change, $t(11) = 4.37$, $p = .001$, by looking longer at the primary object change displays, they did not look differently at habituation as compared to secondary object change, $t(11) = 0.25$; $p > .90$.

Seven-month-olds exhibited the opposite looking pattern. Accordingly, these infants did not differentiate between habituation and primary object change, $t(11) = 0.97$; $p > .30$, but looked longer at the test display when the secondary object was changed, $t(11) = 2.39$; $p < .05$.

Thus, the 9-month-olds responded significantly to the primary object change, whereas the 7-month-olds tended to display sensitivity to the change of the secondary object.

DISCUSSION

The present study started out with the question of whether infants engage in a different weighting of movement–effect instances when they are presented with two instances in close temporal succession. To this end, we habituated 7- and 9-month-old infants to two movement–effect couplings, a grasp/lift event and a touch/overthrow event, each directed at one of two objects, respectively. Subsequently, we exchanged one of these objects and measured infants' recovery of attention when the same set of movement–effect combinations as before was performed, with one of the events involving the novel object. The hypothesis was that if infants preferentially encoded the prehensile action, they should show a stronger recovery of attention to a change in the primary object than to a change in the secondary object that was part of the touch/overthrow event. The results revealed an interesting pattern. Nine-month-old infants behaved according to the hypothesis, in that infants presented with the primary object change event exhibited a stronger and significant increase in looking time as compared to habituation than infants presented with the secondary object change event. Thus, 9-month-olds attended selectively to a change in object when the object was part of a prehensile action. This is underscored by the results from the simple t-tests revealing that infants in the primary object change condition dishabituated significantly when the prehensile action involved a novel object, while infants in the secondary object change condition did not dishabituate when the touching and overthrowing affected a novel object. In contrast, 7-month-old infants obviously encoded the events differently. In this group, there was no increase in infants' looking times in the primary object change condition, but a t-test indicated a significant increase in the secondary object change condition as compared to habituation. The present data thus do not support the idea that 7-month-olds engaged in a preferential encoding of the object involved in the prehensile action. Rather, the data point to a preferential encoding of the object involved in the secondary object change event. One possible interpretation of these results is that early in development infants preferentially attend to movement–effect couplings involving very salient effects, like the noisy falling of the secondary object. Thus, despite infants' ability to encode grasping observed in isolation in object-directed terms (Woodward, 1998), when presented with a second movement involving a salient effect, infants attend more strongly to this second event—which might represent a useful mechanism for learning about new movement–effect couplings. With time, infants will learn about the relations between a specific movement and the consequences that movement has for specific objects, so that they can establish longer-lasting functional relations between movement, object and effect, as for example, that grasping is usually followed by transport, that persons will repeat the grasping movement if the object happens to slide out of the hand, in short that the movement has specific important consequences for future states of the object. Thus, later in development, infants might come to appreciate that some movement–effect combinations, like prehensile actions, are especially meaningful, because they can be used to predict further consequences (such as their mother's grasping of the milk bottle predicts feeding), and concentrate more on these relevant actions, even when they concur with other salient events. This means that infants acquire knowledge about the relative relevance or meaningfulness of different manual actions.

A corresponding narrowing of the attribution of object-directedness to specific movement–effect couplings like prehensile actions seems to occur between 7 and 9 months of age. This could happen on the basis of differential experience with different action–effect couplings. A similar argument accentuating the role of experience has already been put forward by Woodward et al. (2001).

An alternative interpretation could be that the difference in looking patterns exhibited by the two age groups in the present study does not derive from the graded influence of experiential factors, but reflects the functioning of different mechanisms underlying action analysis: an emerging understanding of intentions as psychological states, in contrast to mere behavioural action analysis predominating early in the first year of life. Several researchers have put forward the argument that 9 months might be a special age that marks the development of a first appreciation of intentional relations (Barresi & Moore, 1996; Tomasello, Carpenter, Call, Behne, & Moll, 2005). Tomasello (1999), for example, has termed the phase beginning around 9 months "the 9-month social-cognitive revolution", referring to a major change in social skills that starts to emerge by this time, for example joint attention. This kind of understanding could have led the older infants in the present study to interpret the prehensile action as "purposeful" and the touching/overthrowing event as "accidental", while the 7-month-olds' reactions were primarily driven by perceptual salience. In support of this reasoning, recently, Behne, Carpenter, Call, and Tomasello (2005) found differential reactions in 9- to 18-month-old infants, but not in 6-month-olds, to an adult handing them toys, depending on the adult's intention: when the adult was unwilling to hand over the toy they expressed more activity directed at the toy (reaching) than when the adult was unable to hand over the toy. The authors interpret this finding as implying an understanding of other people as goal-directed agents that is based on infants' understanding of others' psychological states. However, in this study infants could have simply reacted to whether the person had access to the toy or not and, consequently, reached for the toy more often when the person had access. Thus, while it seems obvious that by 9 months infants seem to become more efficient in representing relations between persons and objects, the evidence is not entirely conclusive regarding the assumption that 9-month-olds' action interpretation relies on "psychological understanding" and on qualitatively different mechanisms than 6-month-olds' action interpretation.

Moreover, recent evidence questions the abrupt onset of joint attention skills at 9 months and rather points to a gradual development of social cognition (Striano & Bertin, 2005a, 2005b). This is also in line with the above mentioned finding that other indicators of action understanding emerge before 9 months, like infants' appreciation of "rational" action by 6-and-a-half months (Kamewari et al., 2005). These data would rather suggest that there is a gradual transition in action understanding between 7 and 9 months of age, and at the same time could point to an influence of experiential factors.

Given that most data can be interpreted in behaviouristic as well as mentalistic terms, we would prefer a leaner interpretation based on experience and learning as pointed out above, although possibly the learning of functional relations and the appreciation of intentional relations are developing hand in hand. Future research should aim at specifying the relation between early action understanding and later emerging social understanding.

REFERENCES

Barresi, J., & Moore, C. (1996). Intentional relations and social understanding. *Behavioral and Brain Sciences*, *19*, 107–154.

Behne, T., Carpenter, M., Call, J., & Tomasello, M. (2005). Unwilling versus unable: Infants' understanding of intentional action. *Developmental Psychology*, *41*(2), 328–337.

Bellagamba, F., & Tomasello, M. (1999). Re-enacting intended acts: Comparing 12- and 18-month-olds. *Infant Behavior & Development*, *22*(2), 277–282.

Carpenter, M., Akhtar, N., & Tomasello, M. (1998). Fourteen- through 18-month-old infants differentially imitate intentional and accidental actions. *Infant Behavior and Development*, *21*(2), 315–330.

Csibra, G., Gergely, G., Bíró, S., Koós, O., & Brockbank, M. (1999). Goal attribution without agency cues: The perception of "pure reason" in infancy. *Cognition*, *72*, 237–267.

Gergely, G., Nádasdy, Z., Csibra, G., & Bíró, S. (1995). Taking the intentional stance at 12 months of age. *Cognition*, *56*, 165–193.

Hofer, T., Hauf, P., & Aschersleben, G. (2005). Infants' perception of goal-directed actions performed by a mechanical device. *Infant Behavior and Development*, *28*(4), 466–480.

Johnson, S., Booth, A., & O'Hearn, K. (2001). Inferring the goals of nonhuman agents. *Cognitive Development*, *16*, 637–656.

Jovanovic, B. (2003). *The development of self and intentional understanding in infancy*. Unpublished doctoral dissertation, Ludwig-Maximilians-University, Munich, Germany.

Jovanovic, B., Király, I., Elsner, B., Gergely, G., Prinz, W., & Aschersleben, G. (submitted). *The role of effects for infants' perception of action goals*.

Kamewari, K., Kato, M., Kanda, T., Ishiguro, H., & Hiraki, K. (2005). Six-and-a-half-month-old children positively attribute goals to human action and to humanoid-robot motion. *Cognitive Development*, *20*, 303–320.

Király, I., Jovanovic, B., Prinz, W., Aschersleben, G., & Gergely, G. (2003). The early origins of goal attribution in infancy. *Consciousness and Cognition*, *12*(4), 752–769.

Leslie, A. M. (1984). Infant perception of a manual pick-up event. *British Journal of Developmental Psychology*, *2*, 19–32.

Meltzoff, A. N. (1995). Understanding the intentions of others: Re-enactment of intended acts by 18-month-old children. *Developmental Psychology*, *31*(5), 838–850.

Sommerville, J. A., Woodward, A. L., & Needham, A. (2005). Action experience alters 3-month-old infants' perception of others' actions. *Cognition*, *96*, B1–B11.

Striano, T., & Bertin, E. (2005a). Coordinated affect with mothers and strangers: A longitudinal study of joint engagement between 5 and 9 months of age. *Cognition and Emotion*, *19*(5), 781–890.

Striano, T., & Bertin, E. (2005b). Social-cognitive skills between 5 and 10 months of age. *British Journal of Developmental Psychology*, *23*, 1–11.

Tomasello, M. (1999). Having intentions, understanding intentions, and understanding communicative intentions. In P. D. Zelazo, J. W. Astington, & D. R. Olson (Eds.), *Developing theories of intention* (pp. 63–75). Mahwah, NJ: Lawrence Erlbaum Associates, Inc.

Tomasello, M., Carpenter, M., Call, J., Behne, T., & Moll, H. (2005). Understanding and sharing intentions: The origins of cultural cognition. *Behavioral and Brain Sciences*, *28*(5), 675–691.

Wellman, H. M., & Phillips, A. T. (2001). Developing intentional understandings. In B. F. Malle, L. J. Moses, & D. A. Baldwin (Eds.), *Intentions and intentionality: Foundations of social cognition* (pp. 125–148). Cambridge, MA: MIT Press.

Woodward, A. L. (1998). Infants selectively encode the goal object of an actor's reach. *Cognition*, *69*, 1–34.

Woodward, A. L. (1999). Infants' ability to distinguish between purposeful and non-purposeful behaviors. *Infant Behavior and Development*, *22*(2), 145–160.

Woodward, A. L., & Guajardo, J. J. (2002). Infants' understanding of the point gesture as an object-directed action. *Cognitive Development*, *83*, 1–24.

Woodward, A. L., Sommerville, J. A., & Guajardo, J. J. (2001). How infants make sense of intentional action. In B. F. Malle, L. J. Moses, & D. A. Baldwin (Eds.), *Intentions and intentionality: Foundations of social cognition* (pp. 149–169). Cambridge, MA: MIT Press.

Subject index

For Product Safety Concerns and Information please contact our EU representative GPSR@taylorandfrancis.com
Taylor & Francis Verlag GmbH, Kaufingerstraße 24, 80331 München, Germany

www.ingramcontent.com/pod-product-compliance
Ingram Content Group UK Ltd.
Pitfield, Milton Keynes, MK11 3LW, UK
UKHW011020180926
475701UK00004B/843

* 9 7 8 1 1 3 8 8 7 7 7 3 3 *